MORAL DEVELOPMENT AND MORAL EDUCATION

Unwin Education Books

Moral Development and Moral Education

R. S. PETERS
Professor of Philosophy of Education, London University

London
GEORGE ALLEN & UNWIN
Boston   Sydney

Chapters 1 to 7 first published in *Psychology and Ethical Development*, 1974.
This collection first published 1981.

GEORGE ALLEN & UNWIN LTD
40 Museum Street, London WC1A 1LU

© George Allen & Unwin (Publishers) Ltd, 1981

British Library Cataloguing in Publication Data

Peters, R. S.
  Moral development and moral education – (Unwin education books)
  1. Moral development 2. Moral education
  I. Title
  155.4'18   BF723.M54

ISBN 0-04-370107-8

Set in 10 on 11 point Times
and printed in Great Britain
by Biddles Ltd, Guildford and King's Lynn

Contents

Preface

As a writer I am best known for my *Ethics and Education* (Allen & Unwin, 1966) but I have also written extensively on moral education. My essays on the subject, however, are little known because they are to be found in a large collection called *Psychology and Ethical Development* (Allen & Unwin, 1974) which is beyond the pocket of most students. It seemed appropriate, therefore, to extract these essays and to publish them in paperback form.

My approach to moral education is, I think, distinctive. In the first place my background in the two disciplines enables me to combine both psychological and philosophical material. This is evident in my first two essays, 'Freud's Theory of Moral Development in Relation to that of Piaget' and 'Moral Education and the Psychology of Character'. It is also evident in my two critiques of Lawrence Kohlberg: 'Moral Development: a Plea for Pluralism' and 'The Place of Kohlberg's Theory in Moral Education' (published later in 1978). Psychological material is also used to support the philosophical analysis in 'Freedom and the Development of the Free Man'.

In the second place, while believing in a 'principled morality' as the ultimate goal, I am much more mindful than most of the importance of a 'conventional morality' as a necessary stage on the way to it and of the importance of techniques such as modelling, identification and approval as ways of imparting it early on. This dual emphasis is to be found in my criticisms of Kohlberg's dismissal of the 'bag of virtues' approach, in my attempt to tackle 'Reason and Habit: the Paradox of Moral Education', and in the definitive statement of my views on this issue in 'Moral Development and Moral Learning'.

Finally, though guardedly supporting the use of reason in a 'principled' morality, I am most anxious to show that this is not inconsistent with the crucial role played by feeling. One aspect of this is dealt with in my 'Concrete Principles and the Rational Passions', in which it is claimed that the use of reason is not a dispassionate business. The other aspect is dealt with in the last essay, 'The Place of Kohlberg's Theory in Moral Education', in which a sketch is given of the development of concern for others to supplement Piaget's cognitive stages.

These articles have been written over a number of years but are reasonably consistent with each other. This is because they stem from a definite ethical theory, as must any view of moral education.

Many will disagree with the underlying theory. Nevertheless the articles as a whole raise most of the issues in moral education. It is hoped that they will do something to stimulate further reflection and research.

University of London Institute of Education
November 1980

Acknowledgements

Thanks are due to the *Journal of Moral Education*, vol. 7, no. 3 (May 1978) for permission to reprint 'The Place of Kohlberg's Theory in Moral Education'.

Chapter 1

Freud's Theory of Moral Development in Relation to that of Piaget

INTRODUCTION

In dealing with the vast field of the psychology of morals, Kant's aphorism is particularly apposite: that percepts without concepts are blind and that concepts without percepts are empty. On the one hand there has been a great deal of investigation by psychologists, such as the Hartshorne and May *Character Investigation Inquiry*[1] without adequate conceptual distinctions being made; on the other hand moral philosophers have developed many conceptual schemes which seldom get much concrete filling from empirical facts. The aim of this paper is to explore how psychological theories of moral development might be unified and seen in relation to each other by making certain conceptual distinctions. Such distinctions are necessary for getting clearer about what the theories in fact explain, and for rendering the percepts less blind. I propose to attempt this by setting out Piaget's theory very briefly and by dealing with Freud's theory in relation to it.

1 PIAGET'S CONTRIBUTION

(a) *Exposition*

Perhaps Piaget's most important contribution was to make explicitly a distinction which people who speak of the psychology of morals are too prone to forget. This is the distinction between what might be called conventional morality and the following of a rational moral code. By 'conventional morality' I mean just doing the done thing, or doing what one is told. If a justification for following a particular rule is asked for, the individual appeals to an authority or to what others do or say is right. Usually, however, the question of the validity of such a code does not arise, as in a closed, tight-knit, society, where norms tend to be undifferentiated. By a 'rational moral code' I mean one for which the individual sees that there are reasons, which he sees could be otherwise than it is, which he follows more reflectively.

Now Kant, of course, made this sort of distinction when he contrasted the autonomy with the heteronomy of the will; and Piaget, both in his moral theory and in his theory of knowledge, has a Kantian point of view. What he did was to pour into the mould of this conceptual distinction a rich filling taken from observation of children at different ages. He showed that the distinction actually has application.

Piaget studied the attitude of children to the rules of both marbles and morality and found a correlation between them.[2] At the 'transcendental stage' the rule appears as something external and unalterable, often sacred. At the autonomous stage it is seen to be alterable, a convention maintained out of mutual respect which can be altered if the co-operation of others is obtained. Constraint is replaced by reciprocity and co-operation. A lie is no longer just something 'naughty' which adults disapprove of, a prohibition which goes very much against the egocentric wishes of the child, a command stuck on to a mental structure of a very different order from that of the adult, whose letter has to be adhered to, but whose intention is incomprehensible. It now becomes an action which destroys mutual trust and affection; truth-telling becomes a rule which the child accepts as his own because of the reasons which can be given for it. To summarise the main features of Piaget's contributions:

(i) Piaget insists that there *is* something of the sort which Kant described as morality proper, distinct from custom and authoritative regulation.

(ii) Piaget assumes, so it seems, some process of maturation. There is a gradual transition from one mental structure to another.

(iii) He assumes that this development in the child's attitude to rules is parallelled by his cognitive development in other spheres – e.g. the grasp of logical relations, and of causal connections.

(b) *Comments*

Piaget can be criticised both for what he did do and for what he did not do. Amongst the former type of criticism should be included those of J. F. Morris[3] and D. MacRae[4] who have maintained that many different sorts of things are included under the concept of 'autonomy' which are not only distinct but which also have not all a high mutual correlation. And, of course, much in general could and has been said about Piaget's methods of investigation.

More interesting, however, are criticisms of what Piaget did not do. For instance, he could have investigated whether the transition through the different stages of morality *is* just a matter of maturation, or whether it depends on specific social or family or educational traditions. In a lecture which he delivered to UNESCO in 1947[5] he assumes both that value judgements become more equitable with age and that the development depends on general features of the culture. But he makes no attempt to establish this in any detail. E. Lerner[6] has investigated this question and finds a correlation between the sort of development which Piaget outlined and the social status of the parents and the extent to which coercive techniques of child-rearing were employed.

Havighurst and Taba[7] also studied the moral attitudes of adolescents in a mid-West town and of children in six American Indian tribes and tried to relate them to methods of training, cultural factors, etc.

Such studies are suggestive but very inconclusive. From them three very general observations could be made about Piaget's work.

(a) Piaget's distinctions provide a useful framework for research. The details, however, of this descriptive apparatus need clarifying and tightening up – e.g. his concept of the autonomous stage.

(b) Given that some such transition sometimes occurs, much more needs to be established about the conditions which favour or retard it. These would include a variety of social factors, but of particular importance would be the techniques for passing on the rules of a society. As far as I know, Piaget says nothing about the ways in which parents and teachers help or hinder children in the transition to the autonomous stage.

(c) Piaget says nothing of the extent to which the relics of the 'transcendental stage' persist in the adult mind, and the conditions which occasion a complete or partial failure of the transition to autonomy in a society where such a development is common, and encouraged.

As Freud, so it seems to me, said a great deal in an indirect way about such matters, it is appropriate to pass to his contribution.

2 FREUD'S CONTRIBUTION

Piaget, I have stressed, explicitly made the distinction between conventional morality and following a rational code. In Freud this distinction is only implicit and the features of a rational code are not explicitly sketched.

Philip Rieff, in his timely book,[8] makes much of what he calls Freud's ethic of honesty and of his uncompromising egoism. He suggests that Freud believed in the generalisation of the frankness that is a necessary procedural requirement for psycho-analysis. A man must admit his nature, be quick to detect dishonesty and sham in himself and in others. He must accept his natural needs and have a deep suspicion of 'moral aspirations' such as Freud so often encountered in dealing with middle-class women at the turn of the century. Freud's 'education to reality' and 'the primacy of the intelligence', which he explicitly advocated, go no further than what should be called prudence, rather than morality proper as Piaget understood it. For Freud, on Rieff's view, heralded the advent of psychological man, the trained egoist.

Rieff's account of Freud the moralist, is interesting not only in stressing the cool rationality of Freud's own moral outlook but also in giving a certain interpretation of it. This interpretation is highly disputable. For, although Freud described the principle of impartiality or justice as a cloak for envy,[9] he actually said of himself: 'I believe that in a sense of justice and consideration for others, in disliking making others suffer or taking advantage of them I can measure myself with the best people I know.'[10] This looks very much like the confession of a rational Utilitarian code such as one could find in Sidgwick – or, indeed, in Piaget. It does not sound like the confession of a man who believed only in prudence or rational egoism.

It is therefore difficult to say whether Freud himself subscribed to a rational moral code such as that sketched by Piaget, or only to the cautious prudence attributed to him by Rieff. But, from the point of view of this article, it does not matter. For what I want to begin by stressing is that Freud assumed *some* form of *rational* code, both in his dealings with others generally and in his therapeutic practice. For the aim of psycho-analysis is to strengthen the ego by making unconscious conflicts conscious and by helping people to make decisions of principle with full cognisance of the irrational sources of their promptings and precepts. It is only his basic assumptions both about the distinction between rational behaviour and being at the mercy of the super-ego, and about the *desirability* of rational behaviour, that make his talk of 'education to reality' intelligible and his therapeutic practice square with his theory about morals.

As a matter of fact, the distinctions which he made between the ego, super-ego and id, were ways of making the distinction between behaving rationally and behaving in other ways. He equated the ego with reason and sanity; he says it 'tests correspondence with reality', 'secures postponement of motor discharge', and 'defends itself against the super-ego.' When we ignore the pictorial model which Freud's concepts suggest, we see that their main function is to distinguish between acting rationally when we take account of facts, plan means to ends, and impose rules of prudence on our conduct, in contrast to being at the mercy of the id, when we act impulsively or are driven to act, or being at the mercy of the super-ego when we are obsessed or goaded by the irrational promptings of past authorities.[11]

If we bear in mind this basic conceptual framework we can see, roughly speaking, that Freud's contribution to moral psychology falls under three main headings.

(i) In the theory of the id and the unconscious we find a description of typical occasions when we are deflected from conscious aims, when we cook up rationalisations as a cloak for following our inclinations, when we act unaccountably 'out of character', and when we seem to suffer from a general inability to decide between different possible courses of action, to control our impulses, or to carry out intentions however well-meaning. Such investigations throw great light on what might be called the *executive* side of moral action. I do not intend to say anything more about this side of Freud's work, in spite of its intrinsic interest. I propose to concentrate on the extent to which Freud deals with defects on what might be called the legislative or judicial aspects of morals. This implies something amiss with the sorts of rules which we apply to given cases or with the inability to see when rules fit particular cases. Such defects are to be found.

(ii) In Freud's theory of the super-ego.

(iii) In Freud's theory of character-traits.

These I now propose to discuss.

The Super-ego   The first and obvious point to make about Freud's theory of the super-ego is the extent to which his account of the formation of conscience corroborates Piaget's findings about the child's attitude to rules at the transcendental stage. Freud, it might be argued, went further and showed the mechanisms such as introjection, identification and reaction-formation, by means of which these externally imposed sacrosanct commands come to be interiorised by the child and the standards adopted of that parent with whom identification takes place. This would explain the perfectly familiar procedure of standards being passed on from generation to generation by contact with the earliest admired figures who exert some kind of discipline and provide a model for the child to emulate. Freud, it might be commented, stressed the 'inner voice' aspect of conscience because he took for granted a way of passing on rules which, as has often been pointed out, was prevalent in a patriarchal society where the father exerted discipline in an authoritarian manner, with a lot of *voice*, and where he was taken as the exemplar of conduct. Freud's theory looked after both the negative notion of taking the voice of prohibition into ourselves and the more positive modelling of our conduct on that of some loved and admired figure.

But a closer look at Freud's theory of the super-ego does not altogether confirm this rather obvious interpretation. Even in the matter of the authoritative voice, Freud showed very little interest in the empirical question of how rules were, in fact, passed on, in whether they were in fact taught with a lot of voice. Indeed, he seemed to take the social environment and educational techniques as more or less constant. He was mainly interested in the mind of the child, in the mechanisms of defence – introjection and reaction-formation – by means of which the child either took the parent into himself, in the form of the ego-ideal, as a safeguard against losing a loved object, or took over the parent's reactions to his sexual wishes as a way of dealing with the danger which they represented. He did not simply use his theory to explain how the traditions of a society are handed on by being taken into the child. For most of his theory was used to explain phenomena which were both different from this and different from each other.[12]

On the one hand, he was interested in the fact that some children develop *more rigorous* standards than those demanded by their parents; on the other hand, he tried to explain the familiar feature of types like the arrogant or humble man who have a picture of themselves, an ego-ideal – what Adler called a 'guiding fiction' – which is quite out of keeping with the traits which they, in fact, exhibit. These phenomena, too, he explained in terms of mechanisms which the child employs to deal with wishes in a social environment which is viewed as being more or less constant. The over-conscientious child is one who has turned his aggression inwards; the ego-ideal is the product of narcissism or outgoing love turned inwards. The obsessional and the melancholic exhibit extreme forms of this type of character. In other words, Freud was here concerned with people who had an exaggerated or distorted style of rule-following. This style of rule-following prevents the development towards a more rational way of following rules such as was sketched by Piaget in his account of the autonomous stage.

In his account of the super-ego, therefore, Freud's theory is an important supplement to that of Piaget. For Freud tries to explain why it is that people, as it were, get stuck at the transcendental stage. Some get stuck as a person might who conforms in a colourless way to the standards that are passed on; others exaggerate or distort the standards in question and are incapacitated for rational rule-following later. Of course, in all of us there is left what Freud called a 'precipitate' of parental prohibitions. Following rules in a rational manner can only be viewed as the end-point of a continuum. My point is that Freud assumed some such end-point and gave special explanations for people who got stuck in strange ways a long way down this continuum.

Freud as a Characterologist   Freud's theory of character-traits, too, supports this sort of interpretation. For here again he developed a genetic theory to explain why it is that another defective style of rule-following which impedes the development of ego strength gets laid down in infancy. The picture of the ego wedged between insistent wishes on the one hand and parental prohibitions on the other is again the conceptual framework for the theory. There are, he held, three main periods at which conflicts are likely to occur, the oral, the anal and the genital stages. The techniques or mechanisms employed by the child to regulate his dangerous wishes develop into traits of character. Freud suggested[13] that cleanliness and orderliness were reaction-formations against wishes for organ pleasure; interest in money was a sublimation, money being a substitute object; and obstinacy was a continuation of reaction to parental pressures. Similarly sarcasm, scepticism and food faddism were regarded as oral traits.

I have often been puzzled about what Freud thought he was explaining in this theory. Was he explaining the development of what we call character? Have the carefulness of the calculating determined business man, which is in accordance with the logic of the situation, and the hoarding of the miser, which is not, a similar explanation, the difference being only one of degree? His theory was that anal character-traits are produced by fixation at this stage of sexuality. Did he assume that those who are not fixated but who pass through this stage in accordance with some assumed norm of development, go forward with a minor imprint of orderliness or obstinacy stamped upon them?

In order to get clear about what Freud's theory explained it is first necessary to make some distinctions. By 'character' we can mean, first of all, the sum total of a person's traits like honesty, considerateness, punctuality and so on. We speak of giving a servant a 'character' in this sense. Presumably, too, the famous *Character Education Inquiry* of Harsthorne and May was concerned with the investigation of character in this non-committal sense. For little more was investigated than the incidence of traits like honesty, deceit and so on.

When characterologists, on the other hand, talk of types of character, they usually mean more than just the sum total of traits. They see a certain arrangement of traits which are usually subordinated to one, as in the case of the penurious man. Alternatively, a whole range of traits might be displayed in a distorted or exaggerated manner, as in a pedantic person.

But we can speak of people 'having character' in a third sense, when we speak of a type of consistency which is imposed on other traits by adherence to higher-order principles such as those of prudence or justice. Roback, in his classic on the psychology of character[14] spoke of character in this third sense. So also did McDougall, in what he said about the function of the self-regarding sentiment. Freud's concept of the strong ego is very similar.

Now Freud's theory of character-traits is obviously to be seen in the context of characterology. Indeed, Ernest Jones speaks of his *Character and Anal Erotism* as a contribution to this sort of speculation and notes its literary style.[15] He was surely explaining men who had types of character, men in whom certain traits were so dominant that they provided a unifying pattern. And this, of course, explains the connection between certain types of character and neurosis. Obsessionals, he claimed, manifest exaggerations of anal traits, just as schizophrenics do of oral traits. Freud, I suggest, was perfectly familiar with the penurious character who crops up over and over again in characterology. His genius consisted in spotting the similarity between this pattern of traits and a type of neurosis and assigning a common cause to both. He was put on to this by the findings of his *Three Essays in the Theory of Sexuality* which just preceded his paper on character-traits.

This type of explanation would account not only for obvious types of character, but also, to a certain extent, for the business man who always tends to be a bit more cautious or more optimistic than the facts warrant. There are standards governing decisions like those of the judge, the business man and the examiner. The usual assumption is that people learn these standards on some kind of apprenticeship basis; they gradually manage to master the know-how necessary for making rational judgements about such matters. We do not have to tell the Freudian story, surely, about all cases of caution in business, of rigour in marking or severity and leniency of sentence. But when we note a characteristic bias one way or the other, when there is a consistent deviation in one sort of dimension, it then begins to look as if the Freudian type of explanation is relevant.

Of course, it might well be asked what the evidence is for Freud's speculations anyway. That is another matter, with which I am not here concerned. For it surely presupposes the prior question as to what the theory was meant to explain. I have tried to show that it is to be seen as explaining only types of character, not people who *have* character. Freud's concept of the strong ego would cover what is usually meant by 'having character' together with hints thrown out by people like Abraham about the 'genital character' which describes roughly what I have previously referred to as the end-product of Freud's assumed continuum.[16] Such a person would be one who has not become fixated at any of the previous stages and who has passed through in a relatively smooth way to a more rational way of following rules in accordance with higher-order principles like those of prudence, impartiality and consideration for others which I mentioned previously as characterising Freud's implicit assumptions about a rational moral code.

3 FREUD'S OMISSIONS

Part of Freud's moral psychology, then, can be considered a supplement to that of Piaget in that, both in his theory of the super-ego and of character traits, he gives special explanations of why people do *not* attain the rational level of rule-following. I have argued that in his implicit assumptions about morality and in his concept of the ego he assumes a norm of development towards what might be called 'having character' in an autonomous way – regulating behaviour intelligently, consistently, with integrity and without self-deception in accordance with principles of prudence, impartiality, respect for others and so on. In his special theories he explains how it is that people fail to mature in this way because they get fixated at some earlier period and develop a type of character or because they come to adopt rules in an exaggerated or distorted way at the period of super-ego formation – Piaget's transcendental stage.

But as far as I know there is no positive theory in Freud of the conditions under which this desirable development towards rationality tends to take place. There are, of course, suggestions about very general necessary conditions – e.g. a proper love relationship in early life with a mother-figure, as stressed much later by Bowlby.[17] To be deprived of this is likely to lead to distractability, unreliability, and lack of self-inhibition which are almost definitions of having *no* character, both in the sense of colourless conformity with standards and of autonomous self-direction. But there is no positive theory about *techniques* of child-rearing and the passing on of rules which tend to favour rational development, which Freud treats almost as a maturation norm.

Are there, for instance, certain techniques of child-rearing which tend to create 'fixation'? On Freudian theory 'fixation' is usually regarded as being the product of too much or too little organ pleasure at the early stages. And there are, of course, many cross-cultural studies of weaning and toilet training.[18] But what is the evidence about techniques for the passing on of rules at the later stages covered by Freud's theory of the super-ego and Piaget's theory of the transcendental stage? Plenty is known about methods of child-rearing in the tribes studied by anthropologists; but there is very little established knowledge about what goes on in the various strata of European society. A start has been made along these lines in America[19] and A. N. Oppenheim is at the moment engaged on an ambitious project to remedy just this defect in our empirical knowledge about our own society.

It is pretty pointless to try to rectify our ignorance on such matters by appealing to conditioning theory and to far-fetched analogies between the behaviour of animals and men. For there are many quite different ways of passing on rules to children of which conditioning is only one. So conceptual confusion is only increased if these different ways of passing on rules are not distinguished as a preliminary to investigating what the result is of using different techniques at different ages. The type of instrumental conditioning used on animals, for instance, must be distinguished from that form of training in which rewards and punishments are promised and threatened and not just administered. This, in its turn, must be distinguished from the use of authority which presupposes the use of the voice, but, in giving commands rather than in promising and warning. Then there is imitation, suggestion and learning 'by experience' as well as rational instruction. Given such initial distinctions questions like this could be asked: to what extent do various techniques for passing on rules, when used at early ages where rational explanation and instruction are out of the question, incapacitate the child for rational instruction at later ages? If Piaget is right in saying that there is a correlation between a child's attitude to the rules of marbles and to moral rules as he develops, can any generalisations be made about ways of learning rules which, in general, help or hinder the development towards the more rational stage?[20] Luria, when he recently visited England, reported experiments which he was doing on the use of different techniques for passing on manipulative skills at different ages. He has been studying the use of the authoritative voice, the use of instruction with an explanation, and so on, in these very limited contexts. Could anything be done to supplement Freud's and Piaget's work along these lines? Do some techniques – e.g. conditioning – lead to break-downs, blocks and compulsive habits at later stages? Do they encourage types of character rather than help to develop character? And what sort of training leads to the colourless conformity of the man who never really emerges from Piaget's transcendental stage?

4 DEVELOPMENT OF FREUD'S THEORY

These omissions in Freud's theory are connected with a more general weakness – the lack of any detailed theory of the development of the ego, of rationality in general of which morality is a particular case. In the main those who have followed him, like Melanie Klein,[21] have revised some of the details of his theory about the development of the super-ego – for instance, the age at which it is formed. Others like Horney[22] and Fromm[23] have criticised his theory on the grounds that it is too biologistic and takes too little account of social differences, or that it treats infantile sexuality and the mechanisms adopted to deal with it as determinants of, rather than occasions for, the development of more general orientations.

There are, however, two other lines of development which are particularly relevant to the thesis of this article. There is, first, Money-Kyrle,[24] who claims that Freud's treatment of moral psychology is one-sided because he dealt only with the authoritarian conscience. There is also the humanistic conscience which is traceable back to the 'guilt' experienced in hurting and hating the mother, the first object of a child's love. If the child learns this first lesson, that the good and the bad are often different aspects of the same object, and if he fears lest what is good may be injured by his own efforts or omissions, he has the beginning of a conscience which is more rational and realistic. Whatever is to be made of Money-Kyrle's genetic speculations, which owe much to Melanie Klein, his theory is interesting in that he sees the connection between rationality and what he calls the 'humanistic' conscience and in that he tries to connect different types of 'conscience' – e.g. that of the obsessional, the hypomanic and the hypoparanoid, with different types of falling off from rationality.

There is, however, a second and even more relevant line of Freudian thought represented by Erikson,[25] Hartmann[26] and Rapaport,[27] who have developed the theory of the autonomous ego which was rather embryonic in Freud's writings. Erikson has tried, in very general terms, to map the development of the autonomous ego and to make generalisations about conditions which favour or hinder it. Rapaport has tried to sketch a conceptual model which does justice to the autonomous ego, to show the conditions necessary for the development of autonomy, and to connect his theory with other findings, such as those about stimulus deprivation, hypnosis, 'brainwashing' and Piaget's views on the origins of intelligence in children. This line of development is still exploratory. But a conceptual scheme based on it might help to unify the theories of Piaget and Freud in general as well as in the moral field.[28] It might, for instance, help to clarify Piaget's conception of the autonomous stage. It might also help to connect their investigations with others in the field, and cast some light on what particular investigations in it actually explain; for in this ill-explored field of moral development what is needed more than in almost any other field in psychology is a combination of concrete investigations with conceptual clarity. And this is the point from which my paper started.

REFERENCES

1. Hartshorne, H. and May, M. A., *Studies in the Nature of Character* (3 vols) (New York: Macmillan, 1930).
2. Piaget, J., *The Moral Judgment of the Child* (London: Kegan Paul, 1932).
3. Morris, J. F., 'The Development of Adolescent Value-judgments', *Brit. J. Educ. Phychol.*, Vol. 28 (1958).
4. MacRae, D., *The Development of Moral Judgment in Children*, Ph.D. Thesis (Harvard University, 1950).
5. Piaget, J., *The Moral Development of the Adolescent in Two Types of Society*, '*Primitive and Modern*' (UNESCO, 1947) (quoted by J. F. Morris, op. cit.).
6. Lerner, E., *Constraint Areas and Moral Judgment of Children* (Menasha, Wisconsin, 1937).
7. Havighurst, R. and Taba, H., *Adolescent Character and Personality* (New York: Wiley, 1949).
8. Rieff, P., *Freud, the Mind of the Moralist* (New York: Viking Press, 1959), Chs IX, X.
9. Freud, S., *Group Psychology and the Analysis of the Ego* (London: Hogarth Press, 1949), pp. 86–8.

10. Jones, E., *Sigmund Freud, Life and Work* (London: Hogarth Press, 1955), Vol. II, p. 464.
11. For further development, see Peters, R. S., *The Concept of Motivation* (London: Kegan Paul, 1958), Ch. III.
12. For classic exposition of the theory of the super-ego and ego-ideal, see Flugel, J. C., *Man, Morals and Society* (London: Duckworth, 1945), Chs II-VI.
13. Freud, S., 'Character and Anal Erotism', in *Collected Papers* (London: Hogarth Press, 1942), Vol. II.
14. Roback, A. A., *The Psychology of Character* (London: Kegan Paul, 1928), Ch. XXV.
15. Jones, op. cit., p. 331.
16. Abraham, K., *Selected Papers on Psycho-analysis* (London: Hogarth Press, 1949), Chs XXII–XXV.
17. Bowlby, J., *Child Care and the Growth of Love* (London: Penguin Books, 1953).
18. See, for instance, Whiting, J. W. M. and Child, I. L., *Child Training and Personality* (New Haven: Yale University Press, 1953); and A. Kardiner's various works.
19. Sears, R., Macoby, E. and Levin, H., *Patterns of Child-rearing* (New York: Row, Peterson, 1957).
20. Similar issues are raised and discussed in Harding, D. W., *Social Psychology and Individual Values* (London: Hutchinson, 1953).
21. Klein, M., 'Early Development of Conscience in the Child', in *Contributions to Psychoanalysis* (London: Hogarth Press, 1948).
22. Horney, K., *New Ways in Psycho-analysis* (London: Kegan Paul, 1949).
23. Fromm, E., *Man for Himself* (London: Kegan Paul, 1948).
24. Money-Kyrle, R., *Psycho-analysis and Politics* (London: Duckworth, 1951).
25. Erikson, E., *Childhood and Society* (New York: Norton, 1950).
26. Hartmann, H., *Ego-psychology and the Problem of Adaptation* (London: Imago, 1958).
27. Rapaport, D., 'The theory of Ego-autonomy: a Generalisation', *Bull. Menninger Clinic*, Vol. 22 (1958), pp. 13–35.
28. Rapaport, D., 'The Conceptual Model of Psycho-analysis', *J. Personality*, Vol. 20 (1951). See also Rapaport's, 'The Psychoanalytic Theory of Motivation', in the 1961 *Nebraska Symposium on Motivation*.

Chapter 2

Moral Education and the Psychology of Character[1]

1 REVIVAL OF INTEREST IN 'CHARACTER'

It would be interesting to speculate why particular lines of enquiry flourish and fade. The study of 'character' is a case in point. In the 1920s and early 1930s the study of 'character' was quite a flourishing branch of psychology. It then came to an abrupt halt and, until recent times, there has been almost nothing in the literature on the subject. Perhaps it was the notorious Hartshorne and May 'Character Education Inquiry',[2] and the inferences that were mistakenly drawn from it, that killed it; perhaps it was the preoccupation with something more general and amorphous called 'personality'; perhaps it was the mixture of metaphysics and methodological neurosis centred around the rat. Who knows? Anyway, the study of character is very much with us again as is revealed not merely by Riesman's *Lonely Crowd*[3] but also by the recent study by Peck and Havighurst called *The Psychology of Character Development.*[4] The *British Journal of Educational Psychology* has also, for some time, been running a symposium on 'The Development of Moral Values in Children'.

Philosophers, too, are beginning to emerge cautiously from the central areas where their recent 'revolution' has been concentrated, and have begun to look with chastened souls and sharpened tools at more peripheral problems with which, traditionally, philosophers have been concerned – problems in aesthetics, political philosophy, and in the philosophy of education.[5] They have even begun to think again about moral education. In this field, ever since Aristotle, the training of character has always featured as a corrective to preoccupation with the cultivation of the intellect and with vocational training. A re-examination of the concept of 'character' should therefore permit a fruitful cross-fertilisation between some modern developments in psychology and philosophy, which might be of interest to educators.

2 CHARACTER AND CHARACTER-TRAITS

It is no accident that the concept of 'character' is appropriately used in contexts of individual adaptation; for etymologically the word 'character', like the word 'trait', which is often associated with it, is connected with making a distinguishing mark. 'Character' comes from the field of engraving; hence we talk naturally of the delineation of character. 'Trait' comes from the cognate field of drawing. In their figurative sense, when applied to human beings, they are both used to bring out what is *distinctive* about people.

It seems to me, too, that there is another important similarity between the term 'character' and the term 'trait' which often leads to hyphenation. Their significance is primarily adverbial. They usually indicate a *manner* or *style* of behaving without any definite implication of directedness or aversion – unlike the terms 'motive', 'attitude', and 'sentiment'. 'Trait', however, covers countless manners of behaving. Allport claims that 18,000 words in the English language are trait names.[6] Traits of character are obviously a selection from these – for example traits like selfishness, honesty, punctuality, considerateness and meanness. Such terms, like all trait terms, are primarily adverbial in significance. They do not, like greed or sexual desire, indicate the sort of goals that a man tends to pursue, but the manner in which he pursues them. A man who is ruthless, selfish, honest, punctual, considerate, does not necessarily have any particular goals; rather he behaves in a certain manner, according to or not according to certain rules. And, I suppose, the connection with regulation is fundamental for bringing out what distinguishes character-traits from other sorts of traits – for instance those which we describe as a matter of temperament. Character-traits are shown in the sort of things a man can *decide* to be, where it may be a matter of forcing himself to do something in the face of social pressures or persistent temptations. In this way a man's character is contrasted with his nature. A man just is stupid or lacking in vitality; he cannot decide to be either of these. But he can decide to be more or less honest or selfish.[7] His inclinations and desires, which are part of his 'nature', may suggest goals; but such inclinations and desires only enter into what we call a man's 'character' in so far as he chooses to satisfy them in a certain manner, in accordance with rules of efficiency like persistently, carefully, doggedly, painstakingly, or in accordance with rules of social appropriateness like honestly, fairly, considerately and ruthlessly. Greed is not a character-trait if it means just an appetite for money or food; but it becomes a character-trait as soon as it carries the suggestion that this appetite is exercised ruthlessly or selfishly at someone else's expense, in other words in a certain manner. A craving for a beef-steak, a lust for a pretty girl reveal a man's nature, not his character. His character is revealed in what he does about them, in the manner in which he regulates, or fails to regulate them.

The point is often made that talk of character occurs in contexts of praise and blame. Indeed psychologists since McDougall have perhaps shied off character because of it. To quote Allport: 'Character enters the situation only when this personal effort is judged from the standpoint of some code'.[8] But my guess is that the fundamental connection is between character and some sort of personal effort. The judgement from the point of view of a code comes in because it is largely for his efforts and decisions that a man is praised or blamed rather than for his desires and inclinations. Nowell-Smith, too, stresses the connection between character and praise and blame when he says: 'Pleasure and pain, reward and punishment, are the rudders by means of which moral character is moulded; and "moral character" is just that set of dispositions that can be moulded by these means'.[9] Stupidity and vitality cannot be moulded by this sort of regulation; so we usually do not regard them as traits of character. But this is surely a mistake; for Nowell-Smith's statement that moral 'character *is just* that set of dispositions that can be moulded by these means' suggests that the connection is a necessary one. But we can surely be completely hazy about the spheres in which praise and blame, reward and punishment, are in fact effective; and yet we can talk quite confidently about a person's character. Also there are many 'dispositions' which can be altered by praise and blame that might not be regarded as part of a man's 'character' – e.g. his wants and wishes. There may well be, of course, a close connection between what a person can decide to do or force himself to do by personal effort and what he can be made to do by praise and blame or by reward and punishment. But the connection is a contingent one.[10] And there may indeed be, via the notion of decision, a necessary connection between a person's character and those dispositions which can *in principle* be moulded by praise and blame; for moulding by praise and blame presupposes the decision of the moulded, in a way which something like brain surgery does not.

There is surely the point, too, that if any term is to be linked with social assessment Allport's favoured term 'personality' is an obvious candidate. Allport, of course, uses the term as an omnibus technical term to cover more or less everything that a man is; but such a generalised usage leaves rather high and dry the perfectly good use of the term in ordinary language which, like the term 'character', picks out certain distinctive features of a man. For a man's personality is very much the mask or appearance which he presents to others; a man 'with personality' or 'with a strong personality' is a man whose behaviour is assessed as impinging in certain ways on others. It has not the same suggestion of inner effort and decision as has 'character'. A man's personality flowers or develops; it is not built up by his decisions as is his character. The criteria of assessment are, of course, very different. But certainly to say of man that he has 'personality' is to praise him as much as to say that he has 'character'. But it is to praise him according to different criteria. What Allport means, surely, is that character is connected inseparably with the following of rules. But as one of the most important things to say about man is that he is a rule-following animal, the concept of 'character' should be one of the most indispensable terms in psychology.

This brief excursion into the comparison between the terms 'character' and 'personality' has shown that it is difficult enough to decide what in general we mean when we speak of a person's character as distinct from his nature, his temperament and his personality; but the matter is further complicated by the fact that there seem to be at least three ways in which we can talk of 'character'. We can speak (a) in a non-committal way of a man's character, we can speak of him (b) as having a type of character, and we can speak of him (c) as having character. These distinctions, so it seems to me, are important for discussing matters concerned with the psychology of character, so it will be necessary to elucidate them in more detail.

3 THREE WAYS OF SPEAKING OF 'CHARACTER'

(a) *The Non-committal Use*
I suppose the most common use of 'character' is when we use the term as a way of referring to the sum-total of a man's character-traits. An individual is brought up in an elaborate system of codes and conventions. To speak of his character is to speak of the particular selection of rules which he has, as it were, absorbed in regulating

his conduct both in relation to others and in pursuit of his more personal ends. If a servant is given a character – or was – her future employer is informed of the particular traits which she tends to exhibit, the part of the code which is, as it were, stamped upon her. And it was presumably with 'character' in this sense that the abortive Hartshorne and May enquiry was concerned.

(b) *Types of Character*

In the second way of speaking of 'character', some distinctive pattern of traits is indicated or some distinctive style in which the traits are exhibited. We speak of the anal character, for instance. Presumably this second way of speaking of a type of character is connected with characters in a play. Characters, in this sense, are depicted or delineated either with some dominant trait emphasised or with a typical exaggeration or distortion of a range of traits. Parsimony, for instance, not only is an exaggeration of the 'normal' trait of being careful with money; but in characters like L'Avare it becomes generalised over a whole range of behaviour. This is the sense of 'character' beloved of characterologists.[11] Usually a style of life is sketched which is related to some central trait. Alternatively a whole range of traits is exhibited in a consistently distorted or exaggerated manner. Some of Hardy's characters illustrate this other way in which one can have a type of character; they have a peculiarly obsessive style of following rules like men who are excessively punctual, polite and precise. Freud's theory of character-traits is largely an attempt to trace the genesis of character in this second sense.[12] However, not all 'types of character' present such a depressing picture. There is the 'genital character' of the Freudian school, whose behaviour shows consistency but of a different order. For he regulates his following of rules in accordance with principles of a higher order like those of prudence or respect for persons, and varies them intelligently, making distinctions and exceptions to match relevant differences in the situations in which he is acting. In the case of the penurious man, by contrast, there is no such intelligent adaptation. Similarly the other anal type of character, who has a characteristic exaggeration or distortion of a range of traits, behaves in a way which is irrelevant to changes in situations. The norm-ridden man, like the pedant or over-scrupulous man, always goes further in regulation than the situation warrants. There is, too, the further point that argument and persuasion seem to make little difference to the style in question. And if the rule-following is backed by justifications, they can usually be regarded only as rationalisations. For no counter-arguments or fresh evidence will bring about any change.

The distinctiveness and consistency of the rule-following of the autonomous or 'genital' type of character, on the other hand, is of quite a difficult sort. Such a man will not necessarily be careful with money on all occasions. Indeed he may well present an *appearance* of inconsistency to the observer. He may be frugal in entertaining his friends but more lavish in entertaining his family; he may not insist on tidiness at home but may insist on it in his office. But these variations in rule-following cannot be correlated either with the strength of his inclinations or with the strength of social pressures. He follows rules for which he sees some point and he modifies them to take account of relevant differences in situations; and the point to a large extent, is determined by his adherence to higher-order principles, e.g. that of the consideration of interests. And we usually have to see his behaviour from the inside, from his point of view, before we understand it. Roback, in his classic on *The Psychology of Character*, defines 'character' as 'An enduring psychophysical disposition to inhibit instinctive impulses in accordance with a regulative principle . . . the man of character in the full sense of the word exercises a distributed inhibitory power in keeping with a general principle which subsumes under its authority more specialised maxims'.[13] Inhibition', here, perhaps conveys too negative a suggestion. For 'character' can be shown in encouraging and shaping natural tendencies; it need not always be revealed in their inhibition.[14]

(c) *Having Character*

We come now to the third way of speaking of 'character' which is clearly different from having a type of character. For Kant had something else in mind when he said: 'Simply to say of a man "he has character" is not only to say a great deal of him, but to extol him; for that is a rare attribute which calls forth respect towards him and admiration.' And clearly this sense of character is quite distinct from my first non-committal sense; for a man might well exhibit traits like honesty and truthfulness; yet we might still say of him that he had no character. When Pope said that most women have no characters at all, he was not, surely, saying that they were dishonest, selfish and mendacious. Presumably he was suggesting that they were fickle, inconstant and sporadic in conforming to standards because they were so much at the mercy of their moods and inclinations. Or he might have been suggesting that they took their standards entirely from their husbands or from the clique in which they happened to collect. We speak of integrity of character. A man who has it is not credited with any definite traits; but the claim is made that, whatever traits he exhibits, there will be some sort of control and consistency in the manner in which he exhibits them. He will not give way to his inclinations, be easily corrupted, or take his colour from his company. Similarly we speak of strength and weakness of character which is a way of measuring the degree to which a person can be side-tracked, tempted, coerced, corrupted, or altered by ridicule. Character-traits, in the first and non-committal sense of character, could be merely the imprint of the social code on a man. Such a man, like the Spartans, could behave consistently in a particular social group; but when he went abroad he would fall an easy victim to the corrupting influence of potentates, priests and profligates. Or, like Rousseau, without the constraining influence of the General Will, he would be at the mercy of his vacillating inclinations. But a man who has character, in this third sense, would have developed his own distinctive style of rule-following. This would involve consistency and integrity. It is significant that typical descriptions of men of character dwell not so much on the rules which they follow, the particular traits of a substantive sort which they exhibit, but on the manner in which they follow or exhibit them. When we talk of a person's character a trait like honesty springs to mind; but when we speak of a man as having character, it is something like integrity, incorruptibility, or consistency. These descriptions relate to traits that are necessary conditions of 'having character', but they can apply to different 'types of character' and to a great variety of lower-order traits. They describe the style, not the content of a man's rule-following. And though, as Kant points out, to say that a man has character is to praise him, we can say that he has character but that he is bad. Robespierre and the robber-barons had character. Conversely we can often find something to praise even in a consummate villain if we can apply such 'style' descriptions to his behaviour. A Quaker lady was once told that she would find something good to say even about the Devil. To which she replied: 'Well, he is persistent'.

It is therefore very important for educators to get clearer about what they have in mind when they speak of 'the training of character'; for it is quite possible for different educators to stress this and to have quite different conceptions of an ideal man. They might all be agreed on the desirability of developing traits like consistency, integrity and persistence; yet they might disagree vehemently about which substantive traits were desirable as well as about the type of

character that was to be encouraged. Quaker educators and suppor-
ters of the 'Outward Bound' movement all emphasise the training of
character. But they subscribe to very different conceptions of an ideal
man. It is therefore necessary to look more carefully into the relationship between types of character and the notion of 'having character'.

4 TYPES OF CHARACTER AND 'HAVING CHARACTER'

The analysis of 'having character' already sketched has defined this
notion against two main species of 'the heteronomy of the will', to
use Kantian language. It rules out, first of all, the man who is at
the mercy of his passing inclinations, whose behaviour shows very
little sign of being rule-governed. It rules out, secondly, the man
whose behaviour is rule-governed, but whose rules are those of the
company which he is keeping. Modern typologies of character pick
out men such as these. Riesman's anomic, tradition-directed and
other-directed types of character spring to mind. Peck and Havighurst speak of amoral and conforming types of character. The former
is the psychopathic type who follows his whims and impulses,
regulating them only sporadically. The latter is a man who has no
generalised or thought-out principles about, for example, being
honest. He is often found in stable folk societies and what are called
'shame cultures'. There is, however, an ambiguity about this type of
character. For such a man could be one who has no settled principles
of his own and who acts *in accordance* with a principle such as 'When
in Rome live like the Romans'. Chameleon-like he would adapt
himself to any company that he was keeping out of fear or need for
approval. But he might also, as a matter of *policy*, act on a principle
such as 'One ought always to follow those rules that others follow'
or 'One ought always to follow the rules laid down by the Church,
the leader or the local community group'. We would say of the former
type of conformist that he had no character. But we might say of the
latter that he very definitely had character. Presumably many
Jesuits, army officers and organisation men fall into this latter
category. They would really be 'inner-directed men' though their
supreme principle would always enjoin them to do what someone
else laid down.

Usually, however, men who have character exemplify other types
of character distinguished both by Riesman and by Peck and
Havighurst. Riesman speaks of the 'inner-directed' type of character.
Such a man acts consistently on internalised rules. Typically he is a
Puritan. His moral philosophy is that of Price's or Sir David Ross's

'intuitionism'. He does what his inner voice tells him that he should even though the heavens fall. He is not, overtly at any rate, swayed by his desires and inclinations; he is impervious to what others think of him and cannot be shamed into conformity. He feels *guilt* only about departing from his inner convictions about what is right. His policies are rigid and, if he is an extreme case of this type of character, he will be a compulsive or an obsessive. But he has character all right. Indeed Sargant in his recent book,[15] claimed that such people, together with detached cynics, were the most impervious to systematic brain-washing.

The irrational type of inner-directed character must be distinguished from the more rational type, often called, as by Riesman, the autonomous character. There is, in this type of character, a less rigid type of rule-following; for the rules are applied intelligently and often revised in the light of higher-order principles. If the supreme principle is one such as 'One ought always to further only one's own interests' the man will be what Peck and Havighurst call an expedient type of character. He will be Philip Rieff's interpretation of the Freudian ideal of 'the psychological man' of cautious prudence.[16] If, on the other hand; the supreme principle is 'One ought to consider interests impartially' he will be a Utilitarian, and if it is 'One ought to consider only the interests of others' he will be an altruist. Peck and Havighurst ignore the distinction between these latter two types in their conception of the rational-altruistic type of character. All three types of character are 'inner-directed' and can have character if their behaviour is consistently rule-governed and if they adapt their rules intelligently in the light of their supreme principles.

5   THE COMPLEX TASK OF MORAL EDUCATION

This analysis, though sketchy, should be sufficient to indicate how complex the business of moral education must be. To simplify the approach to it I propose to use a model, though I am well aware that this, like all such models, fails to fit the phenomena at certain places. Instead of conceiving society, as Plato did, as the individual 'writ large', I propose to conceive of the mind of the individual as a focus of social rules and functions in relation to them. A child, if we are to trust Freud, starts life with a strange amalgam of wishes and mental processes which can scarcely be called thoughts because they do not proceed in accordance with canons of logical or causal connectedness. Wishes become wants when social standards defining ends and efficient and socially appropriate ways of attaining them become imposed on this autistic amalgam. With the development of the 'ego' and 'super-ego' these unruly wishes are regulated, shaped and transformed by considerations of prudence and social appropriateness. The child's 'character' emerges as the particular style of rule-following which he develops. And there develop, too, further functions in relation to such rules.[17] There will be, in other words, not only rules which govern the behaviour of the individual but there will also be 'writ small' legislative, judicial and executive functions in relation to them. The following clusters of problems will therefore have to be considered by the educator.

(a) Which rules is it vital for the growing child to absorb? What character is he to have in the first and non-committal sense of 'character'? Next the educator will have to consider what *type* of character should be promoted. This will cover the question of (b) the legislative function, i.e. some procedural principles for modifying and revising rules as well as (c) the question of the judicial function. For the child could learn to apply rules in a rigid rule of thumb manner or could develop discrimination and judgement. Finally the educator will presumably want the child to develop 'character' in the third sense. This will present itself (d) as the problem of developing a stable executive function in the mind of the child.

To discuss moral education within this sort of framework it is necessary to indicate, to start with, the point of view with which one approaches the problem. My concern is for the development of an autonomous type of character who follows rules in a rational discriminating manner, and who also has character. To do this a man must subscribe to some higher-order principles which will enable him both to apply rules intelligently in the light of relevant differences in circumstances and to revise rules from time to time in the light of changes in circumstances and in empirical knowledge about the consequences of their application. The most important higher-order principles which, in my view, are capable of some sort of rational justification, are those of impartiality and the consideration of interests. For these are presupposed in any attempt to justify the rules of practical discourse.[18] These higher-order principles, though pretty formal in character, provide a very general criterion of relevance for justifying particular rules and for making exceptions in particular cases. The ideal is that the individual will develop as Kant put it 'as a law-making member of a kingdom of ends'. He must not only come to know what is in general right or wrong; he must also go beyond the level of what Plato called 'ὀρθὴ δόξα, so that he sees why such rules are right and wrong and can revise rules and make new ones in the light of new knowledge and new circumstances. To do this he must both be introduced to the basic rules of his community and to the higher level principles which enable him to exercise a legislative function.

(a) *The Content of Basic Rules*

The criticism is often levelled against the advocacy of a rationally held moral code that it would lead to moral anarchy. But why should it? For if the higher-order criterion of the impartial consideration of interests affected by rules is applied it will be seen that there are some rules which are so important for anyone living in a society that they could be regarded almost as definitions of a society. For a society is a collection of individuals united by the acceptance of certain rules, and though many of them relate to 'my station and my duties' (e.g. what ought to be done *qua* husband or *qua* teacher) there are also (leaving aside the law) a number of more general rules binding on anyone who is deemed to be a member of the same society – e.g. rules about non-injury, veracity, the keeping of contracts, etc. I imagine that the Natural Law theorists were attempting to outline such a system of basic rules. It would be difficult to conceive of any social, economic, or geographical changes which would lead one to think that such basic rules should be abrogated, though, of course, exceptions could be made to them under special circumstances. Such basic rules are to be contrasted with others which clearly do depend upon particular circumstances. Obviously, for instance, the rule that one should be sparing in the use of water is defensible only in times of drought. The fact that it is diffcult to be sure to which category particular rules belong (e.g. about sexual relations) does not affect the general usefulness of the distinction. Presumably Hare had some such distinction in mind when he begged moral philosophers to address themselves to the question: 'How shall I bring up my children?'[19] The educator has therefore to make up his mind which *are* basic rules and he has to pass on these rules very firmly at any early age.

(b) *The Legislative Function*

Immediately, however, the believer in a rational code runs into another criticism. For it is argued that he is committed to introducing the child from the very start to the reasons for rules, to building in procedural rules which will enable the child to exercise a legislative function for himself. This might lead to endless and abortive arguments with children who treat this as an occasion for outwitting their parents. Now there is no doubt that 'progressive' parents do sometimes proceed in this way and are, not doubt, in danger of developing moral imbeciles as a result. But the believer in a rational code should surely proceed in a rational manner in passing it on to others, and there are at least three good reasons why he is not committed to such a disastrous policy.

In the first place there is an obvious practical reason. Children at an early age, before 'the dawn of reason', are capable of doing considerable harm to themselves and to others. It is as socially essential that they should observe certain rudimentary rules from a very early age as it is individually essential to their survival that they should learn to look both ways before they cross the road.

The second reason is a psychological one; for the evidence from psychologists such as Piaget[20] and Luria suggests that children up to about the age of seven are incapable of appreciating that rules could be otherwise and that there are reasons for rules. Questions about the *validity* of rules make little sense to them. It is therefore pretty pointless making their acceptance of rules at an early age depend upon their seeing that there are reasons for them. And it is also pretty pointless discussing moral education as Hare[21] does by the use of analogies such as that of teaching people to drive cars. For it is probable that most of the formative stages of moral education take place before this sort of rational instruction makes much sense to a child.

The third reason is a philosophical one. It is difficult to see quite what could be meant by developing a legislative function in relation to rules unless the child first of all has some practical examples of rules to work with. And it is no good having understanding of them in the way in which an anthropologist might have understanding of the rules of a strange tribe. He must have experience of rules whose function is to regulate his inclinations; he has to learn what such rules amount to in concrete situations. Legislation as a social process has always developed gradually out of an amorphous mass of custom. Certain rules are selected and more precisely formulated. An analogous development must take place in the mind of the child.[22]

The child, then, has to develop habits of regulation which permit the gradual development of second-order habits of assessment of rules. It could be that the constant barking out of commands, backed by frequent punishment, on the part of his parents, incapacitates him for this. His regulation becomes so associated with fear of punishment that he is rendered incapable of ever developing a more rational form of regulation. And surely 'That is wrong' followed by a slap can function in just the same way as 'Don't do that' followed by a slap. It is not clear that much depends on whether or not the parents use one form of words rather than another to pass on rules; what does matter, however, is what the parent does or says if the child asks why he should conform to what is proposed. For what makes an utterance a command rather than a moral injunction is the sort of backing that goes with it. Commands presuppose authority. Their backing is therefore either an appeal to authority of the form 'because I say so' or the use of punishment, or both. Moral rules are backed by an appeal to reasons such as 'because your sister will be hurt'. Much depends, too, on whether the tone of voice is reasonable or threatening. In other words it is what goes with the form of words, not the form of words taken by themselves that is crucial. It might well be that the 'inner voice' type of conscience, so prominent in the Freudian theory of the super-ego, is a product of authoritarian methods of child-rearing where commands and punishment are much in use. It is difficult to see how, for people brought up systematically in this manner, words like 'ought' and 'wrong' could ever come to be backed by reasons of a morally relevant sort, though they might become associated with appeals to authority or fear of punishment.

The question, then, is not whether to pass on basic rules to children at an early age, but which rules to pass on and how to do so. The child has to learn to regulate his impulses and to understand also that there are reasons for doing so. He has later to develop a second-order habit of assessing rules in the light of such reasons and developing a code of his own. Yet, in the early stages of his learning to regulate his impulses, he is incapable of appreciating what the real reasons for doing this are. This is indeed the paradox to which Aristotle referred when he said:

'But the moral virtues we do acquire by first exercising them. . . . We become just by performing just actions, temperate by performing temperate actions, brave by performing brave actions. . . . A difficulty, however, may be raised as to what we mean when we say that we must perform just actions if we are to become just, and temperate actions if we are to become temperate. It may be argued that, if I do what is just and temperate, I am just and temperate already. . . .[23]

It is only in recent times that the empirical investigation of the effect of various types of child-rearing has been undertaken. Already some interesting suggestions have been made about such matters.[24] It may well be that conformists and 'inner-directed' men of the irrational sort are victims of too many orders, too much punishment, or of too much permissiveness. Rational morality, in which reasons are given for rules, only has a chance to develop if appropriate methods of training permit the *differentiation* of types of rule which is presupposed. What *are* appropriate methods is largely an empirical question which psychologists, in time, ought to be able to answer.

(c) *The Judicial Function*

A man can know what, in general, is right and wrong and also be clear why it is so; but he may be nevertheless what might be called an ideologue – a man with no judgement about the application of rules to particular cases. He may be like this, as Aristotle stressed when talking of the young, because he has no experience of the concrete details of life. But he may have such experience and yet lack judgement like a professor in politics or a theoretical psychologist dealing with his fellow human beings. For rules do not dictate their own application. Situations can be seen in all sorts of different ways. Sending a child to a private school can be interpreted as being unfair, selfish or considerate. Often rules conflict and judgement is required to see in what circumstances a man is justified in making an exception to a rule.

Scheffler and Frankena make much of the contrast between moral education as concerned with the passing on of rules as distinct from 'patterns of action'. But they say nothing about the crucial question of judgement. How it is developed it is difficult to say. Probably Aristotle was right in stressing that it is learnt on some kind of apprenticeship system. And this is surely the burden of Oakeshott's thesis about political education.[25] It is reasonable to assume that it cannot be learnt by drill or sermons. Some suggest that the study of history, by providing a series of cases of men making decisions, might help towards the development of judgement. Machiavielli obviously thought this. Nowell-Smith has recently floated out this time-honoured suggestion.[26] But what is the evidence for this thesis?

Though there is little to be gleaned from a study of psychology about how people do develop judgement, there is a certain amount to be learnt about why they don't. For studies of 'types of character' suggest that some people are rendered incapable in infancy of ever developing in this way. It is as if they acquire unadaptive and unintelligent habits. The Puritan, for instance, whose traits are developed as a reaction-formation against his sexual wishes, will apply his code rigorously and in an undiscriminating manner. Guilt will attach even to his legitimate sex relations with his wife. Similarly the idealist will rig the world to suit his standards. He will be so considerate and charitable that, even when confronted with a really slick operator, he will consistently ascribe to him well-meaning intentions. These are mild cases of reaction-formations against sexual and aggressive wishes which have become magnified into unintelligent rule-following. In extreme cases, of course, the wishes haunt the man as obsessions. His world may become full of possible sources of danger – girls he may seduce, filthy words he may utter, children he may strangle, windows he may jump out of – and so he develops elaborate habits of self-correction. He may indulge in endless routines, self-imposed duties and punishments. He now does not simply apply rules unintelligently which have point in certain contexts; his view of the world is so distorted that he constantly manufactures occasions for the compulsive application of rules. The case of the miser is also a typical example of the development of such an obsession which completely warps a man's judgement.

There is much speculation but little established knowledge about what leads to the development of such reaction-formations. They may result from parental attitudes which contain a strong need for certainty and correctness, from a tendency to load the child too early with responsibilities and decisions, or from unwise handling at the anal stage of development.[27] Or they may result from too much permissiveness on the part of parents. But more empirical knowledge of this sort would only tell us why some people don't develop good practical judgement. It would not tell us why others do. To understand this we would probably have to study the training of judges and administrative civil servants rather than child-rearing techniques. For my guess is that the most the school and home can do in this matter is to guard against permanently crippling their clientele.

(d) *The Executive Function*
We come now to cases where there is the gap between moral knowledge and patterns of action which both Scheffler and Frankena dwell on in their discussions of moral education. How are such cases to be described and how are they to be explained?

From the point of view of description it is important to distinguish between the different types of gap that may exist. When dealing with the legislative function in section 5(b) above the point was made that a child must come to understand rules not in an inverted commas sense or as an anthropologist might come to understand the rules of a strange tribe. 'Promises ought to be kept', for instance, must not simply appear to him as something that others say; it must present itself to him as a reason for doing something in a particular case, for regulating some wayward inclination. And, if the legislative function is properly developed, it is to hoped that he will come to see that there are reasons for having this general rule. Now a man may know what he ought to do in general and have the judgement to see that a rule applies to his particular case; yet he may ruthlessly and doggedly do what he knows to be wrong. He may feel twinges of guilt and remorse about doing it, but he still persists. He wants to do something else much more – e.g. get rich, enjoy sexual experience. This is the case of what we call a wicked man. He is to be distinguished from at least three other sorts of men. There is first of all another sort of man whom we might, perhaps, be more disposed to call evil than wicked. He is not sidetracked by wayward inclinations. He has his own code and pursues it in a determined fashion. But his code includes things like thrashing children and keeping his wife in subjection, which others would regard as palpably wrong. Secondly there is the man of weak will. He knows what is right and wants desperately to do it. He also has the judgement to see what is right in a particular case. But because of his emotional instability he cannot always do it. He is not like the wicked man who wants something else more than to do what he knows to be right. Rather he is sidetracked by emotions like fear, or he hesitates because of jealousy. There may, too, be more recondite explanations of his failure. But he does not, like the wicked man, pursue what he knows to be bad in a consistent determined way. The third case is that of the psychopath who can really only speak of what he ought to do in an inverted commas sense. For although he vaguely understands other people when they talk of what ought to be done, moral language does not really bite on his behaviour. For he cares little, if at all, about doing what he ought to do. Indeed he probably has no consistent policy in relation to his own interest either. The wicked man, on the other hand, is not impervious to obligations; he cares about them only to a limited extent.

How is the case of the wicked man to be explained? John Rawls, I think, gives the clue to this in his most interesting treatment of the moral emotions.[28] His thesis is, actually, primarily a conceptual one in that he wishes to establish a conceptual connection between moral feelings and natural attitudes. He thinks that a necessary condition of the moral feelings of shame, remorse and guilt is the existence of natural attitudes such as self-esteem, compassion and love. We could not, for instance, understand what shame was unless we also had the concept of self-esteem; for self-esteem includes the disposition to feel shame in certain circumstances. Similarly love is exhibited in a tendency to feel guilt or remorse in certain circumstances, as well as in other things. Now whatever the case may be for conceptual connections of this sort there is certainly a very strong case to be made for psychological connections between moral defects in this area and between the absence or weakness of moral feelings and between moral feelings and natural attitudes. The wicked man indeed could be almost described as the man who feels too little remorse or guilt about his actions which he knows to be wrong. Remorse is usually felt for actions which have dire consequences for others; the capacity for feeling remorse therefore presupposes that we have sympathy for others or love for them. Similarly guilt can be felt in relation to a breach of rules that issue either from an authoritative source or which are thought of as being fixed on a basis of reciprocity. The former kind of guilt is expressed in the desire to confess and ask for forgiveness which is a way of restoring the relation of love and trust which this sort of guilt presupposes. The latter is expressed in the desire to apologise, to make reparations, to admit one's faults, which are ways of restoring mutual trust. Such mutual trust and fellow-feeling is presupposed in the autonomous type of morality characterising an 'open' society. It is important to distinguish these types of 'conscience' as Money-Kyrle[29] has stressed in his distinction between the authoritarian and humanistic types of conscience, a distinction which my accounts of the different types of character allows for. But it is also important to stress that both types of conscience presuppose the development of attachment to others learnt in the first instance from parents and developing into fellow-feeling for the members of a peer-group if the child develops from what Piaget calls the 'transcendental' to the 'autonomous' stage of morality.[30] Much of this development must come about by simple imitation and by means of the rather indeterminate process called 'identification'[31] by psycho-analysis which leads to the formation of an 'ego-ideal'. But this is not the whole story; for it does not account completely for the development of sympathy and more spontaneous sentiments. Money-Kyrle, whose theory owes much to Melanie Klein, traces the development of the humanistic conscience back to 'guilt' experienced in hurting and hating the mother, the child's first object of love. But this is rather a dubious hypothesis; for a child of this age cannot feel guilty; for this presupposes that one already has the notion that something is wrong which children of this age obviously do not have. It looks rather like the time-honoured psychological practice of projecting some sort of conceptual connection (the sort that Rawls is trying to make) into the psychological matrix of infancy. Nevertheless there is a strong case to be made for a bond of some sort between mother and infant as being a necessary psychological condition for the development of sympathy. This occurs before the later period when the 'ego-ideal' begins to be shaped.

But this right relationship with the mother at an early age could only lay a foundation for love and, hence, for the later development of guilt and remorse when the child begins to grasp moral concepts. What can be done, subsequent to this, to kindle concern about the consequences of actions in so far as they affect others? How can the example of parents and teachers, which is essential to imitation and identification, be supplemented? My guess is that in our civilisation stories from the New Testament, in which the supreme importance of love is most graphically portrayed, have contributed much. Plato maintained that all moral education must begin with religion in the sense that vivid stories are the most effective and appropriate way of presenting moral truths to children before the dawn of reason. In a similar vein many modern American educators, who are vitally concerned about the development of a 'democratic' habit of mind, advocate the early presentation of the most arresting stories about moral heroes such as Washington, Lincoln and Jefferson. But what permanent effect do such stories exert? Is it similar to that of television serials or different because of the personal rapport which usually accompanies a story? A serious examination of the effectiveness of such age-old techniques is vital if anything concrete is to be established about the moral education of children in our civilisation. For at this stage habits must be formed and feelings awakened which are necessary conditions for rational morality at a later stage. Little is needed to kindle the desire for money, fame, or sexual indulgence which are obvious lures for the wicked man. It is much harder to develop sympathy and imagination so that doing what is right has a positive appeal and is not based purely on fear of consequences. Sympathy and imagination, too, are necessary not simply for caring about rules sufficiently to feel guilt or remorse if they are broken. They are necessary also for the sensitive exercise of the judicial function in making relevant exceptions to rules and for seeing situations as falling under different rules. It is regrettable, therefore, that so little has been definitely established about how sympathy and imagination are developed. For our knowledge about such matters to date comes largely from psycho-analytic speculation and from the hunches of practical men.

So far we have dealt only with the wicked man who knows what is wrong but who, because of the weakness of his sense of guilt or remorse, is too little repelled by the thought of doing wrong to recoil from it. But there are, unfortunately, some men who do not even make the grade necessary for wickedness to be a possibility for them. In extreme cases such people are called psychopaths who are the limiting case of people who have no character called 'amoral' types by Peck and Havighurst. For them moral rules are for ever framed in inverted commas. This, it is thought, is largely due to the fact that they seem incapable of real love and affection and hence of any serious twinges of guilt or remorse.[32] The usual explanation of such characters is in terms of maternal deprivation at certain ages which seems to correlated with traits like 'distractability', 'unrealiability', and 'lack of social conformity' which are almost definitions of having no character.[32]

Weakness of character, as distinct from an almost complete lack of it, is a quite different phenomenon. This type of person knows what is right and wants to do it but constantly fails. The explanation is not in wants which are stronger than his concern to do what is right. Rather he is the man who either seems constitutionally lacking in persistence or who seems to be a constant victim to various forms of passivity. Perhaps he is beset by insecurity which makes him veer from his course at the hint of social disapproval; perhaps unconscious wishes constantly deflect him from attaining his ends; perhaps he is the victim of strange moods. To speculate on the causes of such conditions would be a lengthy undertaking, though, as a matter of fact, psychological theories bear on this problem, if in rather a negative way. For although it is a presupposition of rational action that a man who wills the end must also will the means if he knows what they are, most work done in this field (e.g. by the Freudian school) has tended to explain only why people don't live up to this ideal postulate. As I have argued elsewhere too little thought has been given to the positive conditions of training which are likely to produce a strong ego, to switch from Kantian to Freudian terminology.[34]

But even if we knew the conditions which favour the development of strength of character as well as those which occasion weakness, we would still have to decide to what type of character such strength of character should be harnessed. If this rather lengthy analysis has done nothing else it has at least brought out this point which any educator who talks of the training of character should bear constantly in mind. Indeed the main point of the paper has been to use the analysis of the concept of 'character' to point to the many ambiguities which beset discussions of moral education in general and the training of character in particular. I have tried to show how complicated this task is and how limited and unsubstantial our knowledge is about the process of initiating children into the traditions of rational thought, judgement and determined policies without which the thin crust of rationality cannot be perpetuated. For my model of the mind is, in an important sense, more than a model. Plato once said that philosophy was the soul's dialogue with itself. Similarly a person who has developed a legislative function, as I have called it, is a person who has taken the assessment of rules into his own mind. He has been initiated into a rational tradition stretching right back to Socrates. That is why the model of the educator as an artist producing an end product out of material or of the gardener tending a process of growth are both out of place. For moral education is a matter of initiating others into traditions and into procedures for revising and applying them; these come to be gradually taken in as habits of mind. It is also a matter of spreading the contagion of sympathy and imagination so that such traditions bite on behaviour. But I think that we have little established knowledge about the crucial conditions which favour the initiation into this distinctive form of life.

REFERENCES

1. This paper was read at a conference on 'Education and the Concept of Character' organised by Harvard Graduate School of Education in May 1961.
2. Hartshorne, H. and May, M. A., *Studies in the Nature of Character* (New York: Macmillan, 1930), 3 vols.
3. Riesman, D., *The Lonely Crowd* (Yale University Press, 1950).
4. Peck, R. F. and Havighurst, R. J., *The Psychology of Character Development* (New York: Wiley, 1960).
5. See Frankena, W., 'Towards a Philosophy of Moral Education', *Harvard Ed. Rev.*, Vol. 28, No. 4, Fall 1958); and Scheffler, I., *The Language of Education* (Illinois: Thomas,1960), Ch. V.
6. Allport, G. W., *Personality* (New York: Henry Holt, 1937), p. 303.
7. I am indebted to Mrs Foot for this point which she stressed when replying to an early version of this paper which I read to the Oxford Philosophical Society in March 1958.
8. Allport, op. cit., p. 51.
9. Nowell-Smith, P. H., *Ethics* (Harmondsworth: Penguin, 1954), p. 304.
10. Nowell-Smith was kind enough to read and comment on an early version of

this paper and said that what he says on p. 304 has to be supplemented by what he says about parental smiles and frowns on p. 213. But I am not sure that more detailed specification of this sort affects the main point that I am making.

12. See Peters, R. S., 'Freud's Theory of Moral Development in Relation to that of Piaget', *Brit. Journ. Ed. Psych.*, Vol. XXX, Pt III (November 1960).
13. Roback, A., *The Psychology of Character* (London: Kegan Paul, 1928), p. 452.
14. I am grateful to Sidney Morganbesser for pointing this out to me in his comments on my paper at the Harvard Conference.
15. Sargant, W., *The Battle for the Mind* (Melbourne: Heinemann, 1957).
16. Rieff, P., *Freud, the Mind of the Moralist* (New York: Viking Press, 1959). Chs IX, X.
17. See Peters, R. S., *The Concept of Motivation* (London: Kegan Paul, 1958), pp. 62–71.
18. For attempts towards such a justification see Benn, S. I. and Peters, R. S., *Social Principles and the Democratic State* (London: Allen & Unwin, 1959), Ch. 2; Griffiths, A. P., 'Justifying Moral Principles', *Proc. Aris. Soc.*, Vol. LVIII (1957–8); and Sidgwick's discussion of the principles of Justice, Egoism and Rational Benevolence in his *Methods of Ethics* (London: Macmillan, 1874).
19. Hare, R. M., *The Language of Morals* (Oxford: Oxford University Press, 1952), pp. 74, 75.
20. Piaget, J., *The Moral Judgment of the Child* (London: Kegan Paul, 1932). See also Peters, 'Freud's Theory of Moral Development in Relation to that of Piaget'.
21. Hare, op. cit., pp. 65–8.
22. I am well aware that a rule becomes a legal rule if it is laid down by some one in authority, whatever his *reasons* for laying it down as such. This is one of the points where my analogy of course breaks down.
23. Aristotle, *Nichomachean Ethics*, Chs 3, 4.
24. See Sears, R., Macoby, E. and Levin, H., *Patterns of Child Rearing* (New York: Row, Peterson, 1957).
25. See Oakeshott, M., 'Political Education', in Laslett, P. (Ed.), *Philosophy, Politics and Society* (Oxford: Blackwell, 1956).
26. See Nowell-Smith, P. H., *Education in a University* (Leicester University Press, 1958).
27. See White, R., *The Abnormal Personality* (New York: Ronald Press, 1956), pp. 300–3.
28. In a paper entitled 'Moral Feelings and Natural Attitudes' read at the Harvard Conference referred to above, and worked into his *A Theory of Justice* (Cambridge, Mass.: Harvard University Press).
29. Money-Kyrle, R., *Psycho-analysis and Politics* (London: Duckworth, 1951).
30. Piaget, J., *The Moral Judgment of the Child* (London: Kegan Paul, 1932).
31. See Sears, Macoby and Levin, op. cit., pp. 372–6.
32. White, op. cit., pp. 377–9.
33. Bowlby, J., *Child Care and the Growth of Love* (Harmondsworth: Penguin, 1953).
34. Op. cit., *Brit. Journ. Ed. Psych.*

Chapter 3

Reason and Habit: The Paradox of Moral Education

The debate about whether and how virtue can be taught is a long-standing one in the history of ethics; but right at the very start, when Socrates and Protagoras were discussing the matter, Socrates characteristically made the point that the answers to the questions depended on what is meant by 'virtue'. Is it the 'correct opinion' and conventional behaviour of well-brought-up people? Or is it conduct based on a grasp of fundamental principles? In more recent times Professor Oakeshott has made a similar contrast between two forms of the moral life.[1] A habit of affection and behaviour, characteristic of the gentleman, is contrasted with the reflective application of a moral criterion. There is a corresponding difference in what is emphasised in moral education. On the one hand there is an emphasis on habit, tradition and being properly brought up; on the other hand there is emphasis on intellectual training, and on the development of critical thought and choice.

It is not, however, necessarily the case either that these divergent accounts of morality are completely incompatible with each other or that there can be no *rapprochement* between their different emphases in matters of moral education. Indeed Aristotle attempted to combine both, but was led into a paradox about moral education which resulted from his attempt to stress the role both of reason and of habit. It is my intention in this paper both to combine these two emphases in moral education and to deal with the resulting paradox.

First of all it is necessary to follow Socrates' advice and attempt to get clearer about what morality is. This might be done by examining the uses of 'moral' and its cognates in ordinary language. But it would be a long and detailed task for which there is little time in this lecture; for 'morality', like 'education', means very different things to different people.

Why is it, for instance, that 'morals' suggest something to do with sex and selfishness whereas we speak of 'unethical' conduct on the part of doctors, business men and advertisers? Does 'unethical' suggest the subtle peccadilloes of the more cultured type of man who misses the mark slightly in the way in which a Greek aristocrat might have done, whereas 'immoral' suggests the more brutish plungings of the Roman? 'Morality', too, can cover the crude rigorous code of the Puritan as well as the more rational intelligent code of the scientific humanist. When Freud expressed agreement with Vischer's saying that, 'Morality is self-evident',[2] was he speaking of a crude code whose origin he did much to lay bare in his doctrine of the super-ego, or was he speaking of his own more rational humanistic code?

Behind, however, these vagaries of ordinary usage lies a distinctive form of discourse which has developed to answer distinctive forms of questions. These questions are concerned with what ought to be and with what ought to be done. This is a particular branch of what philosophers call practical discourse. Now practical discourse is not only concerned with answers to questions about what ought to be or what ought to be done. Commands, for instance, are also practical in that they are ways of getting people to do things by means of speech. But they differ from that form of practical discourse in which words like 'ought', 'good', 'right', and 'wrong' occur because there is no implied link with reasons. Saying, 'Shut the door', or, 'Shut up', has a different social function from saying, 'You ought to shut the door', or, 'Silence is a good thing'. Words like 'ought' and 'good' guide behaviour: they do not act as goads or stimuli for reactions. And they guide it with the suggestion that there are reasons for doing whatever is prescribed.

This is not, by the way, what is called a linguistic argument, if by that is meant an argument based on how we actually use words. Rather it is an argument of a Kantian form which attempts to arrive at what is presupposed by our use of different linguistic expressions. Nothing depends on using the *word* 'ought' or 'good', just as nothing depends on using the *word* 'moral' or 'ethical'. But once discourse or thought begins to get differentiated, as when, for instance, we begin to distinguish science from mythology and metaphysics, we can try to get behind these verbal distinctions to see what the differences are in the activities which are so picked out. In the particular case of 'ought', 'good', and other such words, if we ceased to use these words and still wanted to get people to do things by means other than twisting their arms, hypnotising them or giving them orders, we would have to devise a new family of words to do this job.

Morality, then, is concerned with what there are reasons for doing or not doing, for bringing into or removing from existence. But this is only the start of the story; for what makes the reasons relevant ones? Supposing it is said that one ought not to slash people with razors, which is to suggest that there are reasons for not doing this. We inquire what the reasons are and are told that people bleed as a result and blood is red and that is why we should not do it. This would be a reason; but it would not appeal much to us as a good reason because it presupposes the principle that the redness in the world ought to be minimised, which most of us would regard as a somewhat bizarre principle. We would be more inclined to accept a reason like 'it hurts' because we regard the principle that *pain* ought to be minimised as more acceptable than the principle that *redness* ought to be minimised.

It is not my job in this paper to pursue the fundamental problem in ethics of why one such principle is more justifiable than another. I am using this gory example only to bring out the double point that principles are needed to determine the relevance of reasons and that some principles seem more justifiable than others. Our moral principles might be picked out as those which are for us fundamental or overriding in such a structure of rules backed by reasons.

It is manifest enough, however, that in respect of such a structure of rules we can be more or less prepared to justify, revise, or adapt them to changing circumstances. We can guide our lives by a host of rules which seem to us self-evident, or which might be backed up by the very general principle that we ought to do what others do or that we ought to do what X, who is in authority or an authority, says. Or we might try to live by a more rational and thought-out code. For men are creatures of habit and tradition in varying degrees. In a similar way we may be more or less intelligent in the application of rules to particular cases. This is the field of judgement, and whereas some men proceed with fine discrimination, others plod along bone-headedly by rules of thumb. Finally we can do what we should mechanically and with heavy hearts without caring overmuch for what we are doing, like reluctant housewives peeling potatoes. Or we can do what we should with more spontaneity because we genuinely care about that for the sake of which we are acting. In brief, the legislative, judicial and executive aspects of our moral life can be more or less rationally, intelligently and spontaneously conducted.

Professor Niblett, in the first lecture in this series, stressed the importance of making clear where we stand in moral matters. But I do not merely appeal to the august authority of the Dean in order to justify myself in stating very briefly where I stand – the appeal to authority is seldom a good reason for doing anything! The fact is that I cannot explain what I consider the paradox of moral education to be unless I *do* make clear where I stand.

I am a staunch supporter of a rationally held and intelligently applied moral code. Such a code seems peculiarly pertinent at the present time; for, as we have learnt in previous lectures, this is a time of rapid social change, of shifting standards both in regard to general social rules and in regard to activities which are thought to be worthwhile, to which we are introduced in the curricula of schools and universities. My objection to intuitionist and traditionalist positions in morals is not based, of course, on these contigent facts about the social situation. My appeal to the social situation is to support the plea of pertinence. For it is just such facts about changing standards and shifting situations which often lead people who think of morality along intuitionist lines to embrace some subjectivist position and to talk about their feelings or commitments as if morality were a matter of private taste, or falling in love.

I was particularly struck by the peculiar phenomenon of American academics who took what sociologists said about moral relativism so seriously that they would never say that anything was right or wrong; instead they would self-consciously produce their blessed 'commitments' rather like the White Rabbit producing his watch from his waistcoat pocket. Of course this Existentialist type of reaction is to be seen in the context of the massive pressure to conform in America about which so much is said in the literature about the 'other-directed' man. The experiments of Solomon Asch and Stanley Milgram have shown the immense force of such social pressures which can make most men disavow even the plain evidence of their senses. Autonomous judgements requires considerable courage in such circumstances and, if asserted, can have a snowball effect which loosens the chains of conformity. These experiments are particularly relevant to the phenomenon of the teenage culture which we have in our midst. But my point is that the assertion of the individual against such pressures need not take the form of rather self-conscious talk about his commitments. After all some things may just be right or wrong, good or bad. The peculiar pertinence of a rationally held moral code is that it can combine a degree of non-relativeness at one level with a degree of adaptability at another. Let me elucidate in a bit more detail both what I mean and where I stand.

To hold a rational code a man must subscribe to some higher-order principles which will enable him both to apply rules intelligently in the light of relevant differences in circumstances and to revise rules from time to time in the light of changes in circumstances and in empirical knowledge about the conditions and consequences of their application. The higher-order principles which, in my view, are capable of some sort of rational justification, are those of impartiality, truth-telling, liberty, and the consideration of interests. For these, I would argue, are presupposed by the very activity of giving reasons in practical discourse. These higher-order principles, though pretty formal in character, provide very general criteria of relevance for justifying particular rules and for making exceptions in particular cases.

Now just as it is possible for a scientist to stand firm on procedural principles like those of putting his theories up for public criticism, going by the evidence in deciding their truth and not cooking evidence, and yet be willing to change the substantial content of such theories, so also is it possible for a man who holds a rational code to stick firmly to his principles at the procedural level – i.e. the principles of impartiality, liberty, truth-telling and the consideration of interests, and yet to revise what he thinks about the substantial content of rules at a lower level – e.g. about smoking, gambling, or birth-control.

The criticism is often levelled against the advocates of a rationally held moral code that it would lead to moral anarchy. But why should it? For if the higher-order criterion of the impartial consideration of interests affected by rules is applied it will be seen that there are some rules which are so important for anyone living in a society that they could be regarded almost as definitions of a society. For a society is a collection of individuals united by the acceptance of certain rules, and though many of them relate to 'my station and its duties' (e.g. what ought to be done *qua* husband or *qua* teacher) there are also (leaving aside the law) a number of more general rules binding on anyone who is deemed to be a member of the same society – e.g. rules about the keeping of contracts, etc. I imagine that the Natural Law theorists were attempting to outline such a system of basic rules. It would be difficult to conceive of any social, economic, or geographical changes which would lead one to think that such basic rules should be abrogated, though, of course, exceptions could be made to them under special circumstances. Such basic rules are to be contrasted with others which clearly do depend upon particular circumstances. Obviously, for instance, the rule that one should be sparing in the use of water is defensible only in times of drought. The fact that it is difficult to be sure to which category particular rules belong (e.g. about sexual behaviour) does not affect the general usefulness of the distinction. So in a rational code there would be procedural rules which could be regarded as presupposed by the very activity of giving reasons for rules; there would then be basic rules which would be those which could be justified under any conceivable social conditions; then there would be more relative rules which would depend, for their justifiability, on more contingent facts about particular social, economic and geographic conditions. From the point of view of moral education it would be particularly important to pass on procedural rules and basic rules. Hence, presumably, the importance which Hare attaches to the question to which he thinks moral philosophers should address themselves very seriously: 'How should I bring up my children?'³ For in a time of rapid change it is important to pass on both a minimum equipment of basic rules together with procedural rules without which exceptions cannot be rationally made to basic rules or decisions taken about rules of a more relative status.

And so we pass to moral education. But before we do so I want to draw out one of the implications for moral education which is implicit in the position which I have outlined. If one of the fundamental principles of morality is that of the consideration of interests, moral education will be as much concerned with the promotion of good activities as it will be with the maintenance of rules for social conduct, with what ought to be as well as with what men ought to do. Such good or worthwhile activities were emphasised by the Ideal Utilitarians, such as Moore and Rashdall, who tended also to emphasise things like the pursuit of truth, the creation of beauty, the enjoyment of sensitive personal relationships, which defined the way of life of Keynes and other members of the Bloomsbury set at the beginning of this century. They rightly regarded the extension of such activities and of the outlook which goes with them as one of the main constituents in a civilised life. It would be a very difficult task and quite beyond the scope of this paper either to make a list of such activities or to show conclusively why the pursuit of them is in any man's interest.⁴ Nevertheless it is precisely these sorts of activities into which we strive to initiate children in schools. We do, presumably, aim at passing on poetry rather than push-pin. So the promotion of such activities will be as much a problem for those interested in moral education as the passing on of more general rules of conduct.

Now within these worthwhile activities it is generally possible to make the same sort of distinction between matters of procedure and matters of substance which I have made in the case of a rational code. Professor Oakeshott, in his fascinating essay entitled 'The Teaching of Politics in a University', makes a very similar distinction between what he calls the 'language' and 'literature' of a subject. To quote him:

'It is the distinction, for example, between the "language" of poetic imagination and a poem or novel; or between the "language" or manners of thinking of a scientist and a text-book of geology or what may be called the current state of our geological knowledge. . . . Science, for example, in a university, is not an encyclopaedia of information or the present state of our "physical" knowledge; it is a current activity, an explanatory manner of thinking and speaking being explored.'[6]

In such 'languages' are implicit various canons, or what I call rules of procedure, which permit the criticism, evaluation, and development of the 'literature'. The business of moral education consists largely in initiating people into the 'language' so that they can use it in an autonomous manner. This is done largely by introducing them to the 'literature'. And so we come to the paradox of moral education.

What then is the paradox of moral education as I conceive it? It is this: given that it is desirable to develop people who conduct themselves rationally, intelligently and with a fair degree of spontaneity, the brute facts of child development reveal that at the most formative years of a child's development he is incapable of this form of life and impervious to the proper manner of passing it on. Let me spell out these facts in a little more detail.

First, a fair amount of evidence has accumulated to demonstrate the decisive importance of early learning on later development. I refer here not simply to the evidence of Freudians, Kleinians, Bowlby and Harlow who have been concerned, roughly speaking, with the importance of early learning on the development of character and personality; I also refer to evidence produced by more physiologically minded psychologists such as Hebb.

Secondly, both the Freudian theory of the super-ego and Piaget's theory of the transcendental stage of the child's development converge to suggest that up to a certain age rules appear to a child as something external and unalterable, often sacred. Freud went further than Piaget in suggesting mechanisms, such as introjection and reaction-formation, by means of which these external sacrosanct rules come to be interiorised by the child and the standards adopted of that parent with whom identification takes place. It is not till later – well after the age of seven or eight – that what Piaget calls the autonomous stage develops when the notion dawns that rules can be otherwise, that they are conventions maintained out of mutual respect which can be altered if the co-operation of others can be obtained.

No doubt a similar point could be made also about a young child's attitude to the 'literature' of subjects such as geography, history and science. In so far as his minimal concepts of space, time and causality enable him to grasp information handed on which belongs to the 'literature' of these disciplines, he will tend first of all to regard them as pronouncements from an oracle. Until he is gradually initiated into the 'language' of the subjects, by means of which he can begin to evaluate the literature, he will remain in the position of primitive people in respect of their attitude to the traditions of their tribe.

Thirdly, there is evidence to suggest – e.g. from Luria's experiments with manipulative tasks – that the giving of reasons has very little educative effect before a certain age. The explanations given by adults bite very little into the child's behaviour, though commands do have an effect at an earlier age.

Nevertheless, in spite of the fact that a rational code of behaviour and the 'language' of a variety of activities is beyond the grasp of young children, they can and must enter the palace of Reason through the courtyard of Habit and Tradition. This is the paradox of moral education which was first put so well by Aristotle in Book 2 of his *Nicomachean Ethics.*

The problem of moral education is that of how the necessary habits of behaviour and the deep-rooted assumptions of the 'literature' of various forms of good activities can be acquired in a way which does not stultify the development of a rational code or the mastery of the 'language' of activities at a later stage.

I am assuming, by the way, like Aristotle, that children gradually acquire these desirable forms of life by some on-the-spot apprenticeship system. I am also assuming something about the factor which I previously picked out when I stressed the spontaneous enjoyment that goes with such a form of life. Spinoza put this in a very general way when he declared that, 'Blessedness is not the reward of right-living; it is the right living itself; nor should we rejoice in it because we restrain our desires, but, on the contrary, it is because we rejoice in it that we restrain them.'[6] In the jargon of modern psychology this is to say that a rational code and worthwhile activities are intrinsically not extrinsically motivated.

Now education, at any rate at later levels, consists largely in initiating people into this form of life – in getting others on the inside of activities so that they practise them simply for the intrinsic satisfactions that they contain and for no end which is extrinsic to them. That is why one gets so impatient with the endless talk about the aims of education and the modern tendency to speak about education in the economic jargon of 'investment' and 'commodity'. No one, of course, would deny that many skills and much information have to be passed on to sustain and increase productivity in an industrial society; it is also the case that if money has to be raised from hard-headed business men or from an over-taxed and materialistically minded public, the instrumental aspects of what goes on in schools and universities may have to be stressed. But anyone who reflects must ask questions about the point of keeping the wheels of industry turning. And the answer is not simply that it is necessary for survival or 'living' – whatever that means. It is necessary for the maintenance and extension of a civilised life whose distinctive outlook and activities are those which are passed on in schools and universities. In such institutions there is no absolute distinction between teacher and learner. It is a matter of degree of skill, knowledge, insight and experience within a common form of life. So there is an important sense in which 'life', by which is usually meant that which goes on outside the class-room, is for the sake of education, not education for life. This point was well made by the philosopher who was castigated by the Marxist for trying to understand the world rather than to change it. When asked what he proposed to *do* when he had achieved the classless society the Marxist admitted that he might then get round to the sort of thing that the philosopher was doing. To which the philosopher replied: 'I guess I am ahead of my time then!'

Now anyone who has managed to get on the inside of what is passed on in schools and universities, such as science, music, art, carpentry, literature, history and athletics, will regard it as somehow ridiculous to be asked what the point of his activity is. The mastery of the 'language' carries with it its own delights, or 'intrinsic motivation', to use the jargon. But for a person on the *outside* it may be difficult to see what point there is in the activity in question. Hence the incredulity of the uninitiated when confronted with the rhapsodies of the mountain-climber, musician or golfer. *Children* are to a large extent in the position of such outsiders. The problem is to introduce them to a civilised outlook and activities in such a way that they can get on the inside of those for which they have aptitude.

The same sort of problem can be posed in the case of their attitude to rules of conduct. Is it the case that children have to be lured by irrelevant incentives or goaded by commands so that they acquire the basic habits of conduct and the 'literature' of the various activities without which they cannot emerge to the later stage? Is it the case that we have to use such irrelevant 'extrinsic' techniques to get children going so that eventually they can take over for themselves, without needing any longer such extrinsic incentives or goads? Or does the use of such extrinsic techniques militate against intelligent, spontaneous, and intrinsically directed behaviour later on?

It might be argued, for instance, that the various maturation levels bring with them the possibility of a variety of intrinsic motivations falling under concepts such as competence,[7] mastery and curiosity. Then there is the ubiquitous role of love and trust; for psychoanalysts such as Bowlby suggest that the existence of a good relationship of love and trust between parent and child during the early years is a necessary condition for the formation of any enduring and consistent moral habits.[8] Whether love, the withdrawal of love, approval and disapproval, constitute extrinsic or intrinsic motivations in respect to the development of habits is too complicated a question to consider here. Nevertheless it may well be that the use of such intrinsic as distinct from extrinsic motivations may be crucial in determining the type of habits that are formed. For the formation of *some* types of habit may not necessarily militate against adaptability and spontaneous enjoyment. However, it is often thought that, because of the very nature of habits, dwelling in the courtyard of Habit incapacitates a man for life in the palace of Reason. I now propose to show both why this need not be the case and why people can be led to think that it must be the case.

Aristotle was not alone in stressing the importance of habits in moral training. There is William James's celebrated chapter on the subject in which the purple passage occurs:

'Could the young but realise how soon they will become mere walking bundles of habits, they would give more heed to their conduct while in the plastic state. . . . Every smallest stroke of virtue or of vice leaves its never so little scar. The drunkard Rip Van Winkle, in Jefferson's play, excuses himself for every fresh dereliction by saying, "I won't count this time!" Well! he may not count it, and a kind Heaven may not count it: but it is being counted none the less.

Down among his nerve cells and fibres the molecules are counting it, registering and storing it up to be used against him when the next temptation comes. Nothing we ever do is, in strict scientific literalness, wiped out.'[9]

The evidence from early learning reinforces James's graphic, if depressing, homily. The formation of sound moral habits in respect of, for instance, what I have called basic moral rules might well be a necessary condition of rational morality. It can, however, seem to be antagonistic to rational morality because of an interesting sort of conceptual confusion and because of the development, through a variety of causes, of specific types of habit. I will deal first with the conceptual issue and then proceed to the more empirical one.

What, then, do we mean by 'habits' and is there any necessary contradiction in stressing the importance of habit in moral matters while, at the same time, stressing the intelligent adaptability which is usually associated with reason, together with the spontaneous enjoyment associated with civilised activities?

The first thing to get clear about is that habits, like motives or emotions, are not as it were part of the furniture of the mind in the way in which the yellow, green and black are part of a snooker set. These terms are higher-order ones by means of which we say all sorts of extra things about people's actions, feelings and so on. 'Habit' is a term which we use to say extra things about people's *actions*. They must pick out the sorts of things that we could, in principle, have reasons for doing and the sorts of thing that, in principle, we could stop doing if we tried. It would be odd to talk about a heart-beat or a nervous tic as a habit. Forms of passivity such as stomach-aches or feelings of pity or fear are not properly described as habits either.

When we describe an action as a 'habit' we suggest, first of all, that the man has done this very thing before and that he will probably do it again. We are postulating a tendency to act in this way. 'Habit' also carries with it the suggestion not only of repetition but also of the ability to carry out the action in question 'automatically'. A man can automatically stir his tea or puff his pipe while discussing the latest developments in Cuba and if you ask him whether he puts his left sock on before his right, or vice versa, he may say that he requires notice of that question. And if you ask him to pay attention so that he can tell you in what order he makes a series of movements when hitting a good drive at golf he will probably put the ball into the neighbouring wood. This is not a tip for the life-man; it is support for the Duke of Wellington who proclaimed: 'Habit a second nature! Habit is ten times nature!' The art of living consists, to a large extent, in reducing most things that have to be done to habit; for then the mind is set free to pay attention to things that are interesting, novel and worthwhile.

Of course not all things done automatically are necessarily habits. If a man hears a scrabbling at the window and sees what he takes to be an escaped gorilla peering at him, he may 'automatically' dial 999 while wondering where he has put the bananas. But we would not describe dialling 999 as a habit. Automatic writing need not be one of a person's habits; for 'automatically' picks out only part of what is meant by 'habit' and only in the weak sense that it suggests that is the sort of thing that a man *can* do automatically. Getting up at eight does not cease to be one of a person's habits if, on occasions, he pays careful heed to what he is doing and leaps out of bed briskly the moment the alarm-clock tolls the knell of the dawning day.

What are the implications of this analysis for the development of adaptability which is the hallmark of skilled and civilised activities? What we call a skill presupposes a number of component habits. A fielder at cricket, for instance, may be very skilful and show great intelligence in running a man out by throwing the ball to the bowler rather than to the wicket-keeper. But to do this he would have to bend down, pick the ball up, and contort his body with his eye partly on the ball and partly on the position of the batsmen. But unless these component actions were more or less habits he would not be able to concentrate on using them in the service of the higher strategy of the game. But – and this is the important point – all these component actions would have to be capable of being performed with a degree of plasticity to permit co-ordination in a wide variety of very different overall actions. The concept of 'action' is 'open-ended' in many dimensions. We could describe the man as moving his arm, as throwing the ball at the wicket, or throwing it at the bowler's end, or as running the batsman out, depending on the aspect under which the fielder conceived what he was doing. In what we call 'mechanical' actions a man will always conceive the movements as leading up in a stereotyped way to a narrowly conceived end. In intelligent actions the component actions are conceived of as variable and adaptable in the light of some more generally conceived end. The teachers who have taught me most about golf and about philosophy are those who have insisted on conveying an overall picture of the performance as a whole in which the particular moves have to be practised under the aspect of some wider conception, instead of concentrating either on drilling me in moves which are conceived in a very limited way or going simply for the overall picture without bothering about practising the component moves.

Now the type of habits which would count as moral habits *must* be exhibited in a wide range of actions in so far as actions are thought to be constituted by the sorts of movements of the body that are usually associated with skills. Consider, for instance, the range of such actions that can fall under the concept of theft or malice. What makes an action a case of theft is that it must be conceived of as involving appropriating, without permission, something that belongs to someone else. A child, strictly speaking, cannot be guilty of theft, who has not developed the concept of himself as distinct from others, of property, of the granting of permission, etc. It takes a long time to develop such concepts. In the early years, therefore, parents may think that they are teaching their children not to steal, whereas in fact they are doing no such thing. They may be teaching the child something else, e.g. to inhibit actions of which authority figures disapprove, or to inhibit a narrowly conceived range of movements. At the toilet training stage, for instance, children may pick up very generalised and often unintelligent habits – e.g. punctilious conformity to rules, unwillingness to part with anything that is theirs. But this is not what the parents were trying to teach them. For the children probably lack the concepts which are necessary for understanding what the parents *think* that they are teaching them, namely the rule of cleanliness. To learn to act on rules forbidding theft, lying, breaking promises, etc., is necessarily an open-ended business requiring intelligence and a high degree of social sophistication. For the child has to learn to see that a vast range of very different actions and performances can fall under a highly abstract rule which makes them all examples of a type of action. If the child has really learnt to act on a rule it is difficult to see how he could have accomplished this without insight and intelligence. He might be drilled or forced to act in *accordance with* a rule; but that is quite different from learning to act *on* a rule.

So it seems as if the paradox of moral education is resolved. For there is no *necessary* contradiction between the use of intelligence and the formation of habits. How then does the antithesis between the two, which is frequently made, come about? Partly, I think, through the existence of certain explanatory expressions such as 'out of habit', and partly because of certain empirical facts about a special class of habits.

To take the point about explanatory expressions first. In explaining particular actions or courses of action we often use the phrase 'out of habit', 'through force of habit', or 'that is a matter of sheer habit'. This type of phrase does not simply suggest that what the man is doing is a habit in the sense that he has a tendency to do this sort of thing and that he can do it automatically. It also implies that in this case:

(i) The man has no reason for doing it which would render the action other than one conceived in a limited way. He could of course be raising his arm to attract someone's notice. He might indeed produce such a reason for doing it if asked. But to say that he raised his arm on this occasion 'out of habit' or through 'force of habit' is to deny that, on this occasion, such a reason which he might have, was *his* reason. Raising his arm *simpliciter*, we are saying, is just the sort of thing that he tends to do.

(ii) The clash with the idea of spontaneity, which is also often associated with 'habit', comes in also because to say that a man cleans his teeth or washes up 'out of habit' or 'through force of habit' is to exclude the possibility that there is any enjoyment in it for him, that he is doing it for pleasure, for what he sees in it as distinct from what he sees it leading on to. It is, in other words, to rule out intrinsic motivation. It is to explain what he does, roughly speaking, in terms of the law of exercise, and to rule out any variant of the law of effect.

It would follow from this that the things which we are wont to do out of habit tend to be pretty stereotyped and narrowly conceived things, which are usually fired off by familiar stimuli. Often a superficially similar cue can release a whole train of such stereotyped movements when the circumstances are relevantly dissimilar. I remember the ghastly sensation of trying to ride a motor-bike and side-car after being trained on a motor-bike. As I automatically banked my body over and the bike went inexorably towards the gorse-bushes on the moor that stretched beside the road, my brother yelled at me: 'Imagine that you are steering a ship, not riding a motor-cycle.' He was thereby following the correct educative procedure which I have referred to above in order to release me from the force of habit.

Given, then, that the explanation 'out of habit' or 'from force of habit' rules out the possibility of a further extrinsic end by reference to which an action could be deemed to be intelligent and given that 'out of habit' also rules out explanations in terms of pleasure, enjoyment, or any kind of intrinsic motivation, it is obvious enough why the intelligent adaptability of a rational code as well as spontaneous delight in practising it and in pursuing worthwhile activities are in stark opposition to things that are done 'out of habit'. But, as

I have tried to show, they are not so opposed to habits as mere descriptions of types of action. Habits need not be exercised out of force of habit.

The fact, however, that they very often *are* brings me to my empirical point, which is that there are a great number of things which we do in fact do out of habit, and this is essential if our minds are to be set free to attend to other things. Remember the Duke of Wellington. It is also the case that in some people whom, in extreme cases, we describe as compulsives, the force of habit is so strong that it militates against intelligent performance and disrupts the rest of a man's life. Tidiness and cleanliness are in general sound moral habits because they save time and health and permit efficient and intelligent performance of countless other things. But if a woman is so obsessed with them that she tries to impress the stamp of the operating theatre on the nursery and bedroom of young children, she may well have reached the point where her habits disrupt not only her domestic bliss but also her own capacity for intelligent adaptation and for enjoyment of things that are worth enjoying.

And so we stand at the door of the nursery which is the gateway to moral education. For it is here, in all probability, that the pattern of character-traits and the manner of exercising them is laid down. It is here that habits are first formed in a manner which may lead to the development of compulsives, obsessives, Puritans, and impractical ideologues. To explain how this probably happens would involve a careful examination of cognitive development and the role of extrinsic and intrinsic motivation in childhood. I could not begin to tackle this vast subject in this paper. I have only tried to explain and to resolve the *theoretical* paradox of moral education, not to develop a positive theory of rational child-rearing.

Aristotle put the matter very well when he said:

'But the virtues we get by first exercising them, as also happens in the case of the arts as well. For the things we have to learn before we can do them, we learn by doing them, e.g. men become builders •by building and lyre players by playing the lyre; so do we become just by doing just acts, temperate by doing temperate acts, brave by doing brave acts. This is confirmed by what happens in the State; for legislators make the citizens good by forming habits in them . . . by doing the acts that we do in our transactions with other men we become just or unjust, and by doing the acts that we do in the presence of danger, and by habituating ourselves to feel fear or confidence, we become brave or cowardly. . . . It makes no small difference then, whether we form habits of one kind or another from our very youth; it makes a great difference or rather all the difference. . . .'[10]

But from the point of view of moral education it makes all the difference, too, at what age and in what manner such habits are formed, especially under what aspect particular acts are taught. For it is only if habits are developed in a certain kind of way that the paradox of moral education can be avoided in practice. This is a matter about which psychologists and practical teachers will have much more to say than philosophers. For I have only tried to resolve the theoretical paradox of moral education in a theoretical manner.

Bacon once said that the discourse of philosophers is like the stars; it sheds little light because it is so high. But when it is brought nearer the earth, as I hope it has been in this paper, it still can only shed light on where empirical research needs to be done and where practical judgements have to be made. It is no substitute for either. I hope that subsequent papers in this series will enrich our knowledge and increase our wisdom in relation to these more mundane matters.

REFERENCES

1. Oakeshott, I. M., 'The Tower of Babel', in *Rationalism in Politics* (London: Methuen, 1962), pp. 59–79.
2. See Jones, E., *Sigmund Freud, Life and Work* (London: Hogarth Press, 1955). Vol. II, p. 463.
3. Hare, R., *The Language of Morals* (Oxford: Oxford University Press, 1952). pp. 74–5.
4. See Griffiths, A. P. and Peters, R. S., 'The Autonomy of Prudence', *Mind*, Vol. LXXI (April 1962), pp. 161–80.
5. Oakeshott, M., *Rationalism in Politics and Other Essays* (London: Methuen, 1962), pp. 308, 311.
6. Spinoza, *Ethics*, Pt V., Prop. XLII.
7. See, for instance, White R., 'Competence and the Psychosexual Stages of Development,' in *Nebraska Symposium on Motivation* (1960).
8. See Peters, R. S., 'Moral Education and the Psychology of Character', *Philosophy* (January 1962).
9. James, W., *Principles of Psychology* (Macmillan, 1891), p. 127.
10. Aristotle, *Nicomachean Ethics*, Bk II, Chs 3, 4.

Chapter 4

Concrete Principles and the Rational Passions

INTRODUCTION

In education content is crucial. There is some point in raising aloft the romantic banners of 'development', 'growth', and 'discovery' when children are being bored or bullied. Romanticism is always valuable as a protest. But another sort of trouble starts when romantics themselves get into positions of authority and demand that children shall scamper around being 'creative' and spontaneously 'discovering' what it has taken civilised man centuries to understand. Some synthesis has to be worked out between established content and individual inventiveness. The basis for such a synthesis is to be found mainly in those public historically developed modes of experience whose immanent principles enable individuals to build up and revise an established content and to make something of themselves within it. In science, for instance, merely learning a lot of facts is a weariness of the spirit; but a Robinson Crusoe, untutored in a scientific tradition, could not ask a scientific question, let alone exhibit 'creativity'. Originality is possible only for those who have assimilated some content and mastered the mode of experience, with its immanent principles, by means of which this content has been established and repeatedly revised.

The same sort of Hegelian progression is detectable in morality. 'Morality' to many still conjures up a 'code' prohibiting things relating to sex, stealing and selfishness. The very word 'code' suggests a body of rules, perhaps of an arbitrary sort, that all hang together but that have no rational basis. To others, however, morality suggests much more individualistic and romantic notions, such as criterionless choices, individual autonomy and subjective preferences. Whether one experiences anguish in the attempt to be 'authentic', produces one's commitment, like the White Rabbit producing his watch from his waistcoat pocket, or proclaims, like Bertrand Russell, that one simply does not *like* the Nazis, the picture is roughly the same – that of the romantic protest. Synthesis must be sought by making explicit the mode of experience which has gradually enabled civilised people to distinguish what is a matter of morals from what is a matter of custom or law, and which has enabled them to revise and criticise the code in which they have been brought up, and gradually to stand on their own feet as autonomous moral beings. This they could never have done without a grasp of principles.

It is the details of this sort of synthesis that I propose to explore in this essay as a preliminary to discussing moral education; for it is no good talking about moral education until we have a more determinate conception of what is involved in being 'moral'. Because they are uncertain about this, many well-meaning parents and teachers are hamstrung in their attempts at moral education. If they incline toward the code conception, they tend to be authoritarian in their approach; if, on the other hand, they favour some variant of the romantic reaction, they may expect that children will go it alone and decide it all for themselves. A more adequate view of morality should reveal the proper place for both authority and self-directed learning in moral education. But I shall not have space to deal with details of such educational procedures in this essay – only to explore a middle road between these two extreme positions and to view the general contours of moral education from this vantagepoint.

1 THE FUNCTIONS OF PRINCIPLES

There are some, like Alasdair MacIntyre, who seem to hold that we have no middle way between allegiance to a surviving code and some kind of romantic protest. For, it is argued, moral terms such as 'good' and 'duty', once had determinate application within a close-knit society with clear-cut purposes and well-defined roles; but now, because of social change, they have broken adrift from these concrete moorings. A pale substitute is left in generalised notions such as 'happiness' instead of concrete goals, and duty for duty's sake instead of duties connected with role performances that were manifestly related to the goals of the community. So we have a kind of moral schizophrenia in the form of irresolvable conflicts between 'interest' and 'duty' and no determinate criteria for applying these general notions, because their natural home has passed away. It is no wonder, on this view, that those who have not been brought up in one of the surviving tribalisms make such a fuss about commitment and criterionless choice; for there is nothing else except those ancient realities to get a grip on.

(a) *The Emergence of a Rational Morality Based on Principles*
But even if this is how concepts such as 'good' and 'duty' originated, why this nostalgic fixation on those stuffy, self-contained little communities, such as Sparta, where they could be unambiguously applied? Could not one be equally impressed by the Stoic concept of a citizen of the world, by the law of nations forged by the Roman jurisprudents, and by the labours of lawyers such as Grotius to hammer out laws of the sea against piracy? The point is that both science and a more rational, universalistic type of morality gradually emerged precisely because social change, economic expansion and conquest led to a clash of codes and to conflict between competing views of the world. Men were led to reflect about which story about the world was true, which code was correct. In discussing and reflecting on these matters they came to accept higher-order principles of a procedural sort for determining such questions.

MacIntyre, it is true, applauds those like Spinoza who drew attention to values connected with freedom and reason. He admits the supreme importance of truth-telling; he notes the massive consensus about basic rules for social living first emphasised by the Natural Law theorists, which H. L. Hart has recently revived as the cornerstone of a moral system. Why then is he so unimpressed by this consensus that he gives such a one-sided presentation of the predicament of modern man? Mainly, so it seems, because an appeal to such principles and basic rules cannot give specific guidance to any individual who is perplexed about what he ought to do.

(b) *Difficulties About Concrete Guidance*
Two connected difficulties are incorporated in this type of objection to principles. The first, already mentioned, is that no concrete guidance can be provided by them for an individual who wants to know what he ought to do. This is usually illustrated by the case of the young man who came to Sartre wanting guidance about whether he should stay at home and look after his aged mother or go abroad and join the Free French. How could an appeal to principles help him? Well, surely he only had a problem because he already acknowledged duties connected with his status as a son and as a citizen. Would Sartre have said to him 'You have to decide this for yourself'

if the alternative to joining the Free French had been presented as staying at home and accepting bribes from the Germans for information? And surely if what is claimed to be missing is a principle for deciding between these duties, there are principles which would rule out some reasons which he might give for pursuing one of the alternatives. Supposing, for instance, he said that he was inclined toward going abroad because he wanted to determine precisely the height of St Paul's Cathedral. Would Sartre have applauded his exercise of criterionless choice?

The existentialist emphasis on 'choice' is salutary, of course, in certain contexts. It is important, for instance, to stress man's general responsibility for the moral system which he accepts. This needs to be said against those who smugly assume that it is just there to be read off. It needs to be said, too, in the context of atrocities such as Belsen. It also emphasises the extent to which character is destiny and the role which choices play in shaping the individual's character. In this kind of development, conflict situations are particularly important, and if fundamental principles conflict there is not much more that one can say than that the individual must make up his own mind or use his 'judgement'. But we do not decide on our fundamental principles such as avoiding pain or being fair; still less do we 'choose' them. Indeed, I would feel very uneasy in dealing with a man who did. And why should a moral theory be judged by its capacity to enable the individual to answer the question 'What ought I to do now?' as distinct from the question 'What, in general, are there reasons for doing?' Do we expect casuistry from a moral philosopher or criteria for making up our own minds?

The more important difficulty is the one MacIntyre has in mind, that fundamental principles such as 'fairness' or 'considering people's interests' give us such abstract criteria that they are useless because they always have to be interpreted in terms of a concrete tradition. I am very sympathetic to this objection, but I think that it also applies in varying degrees to all rational activities. To take a parallel: all scientists accept some higher-order principle such as that one ought to test competing hypotheses by comparing the deduced consequences with observations. But this does not give them concrete guidance for proceeding. It has to be interpreted. To start with, what is to count as an observation? The amount of social tradition and previous theory built into most observation procedures, especially in the social sciences, is obvious enough. And how is the importance of one set of observations to be assessed in relation to others? This is not unlike saying in the moral case: Consider impartially the suffering of people affected by a social practice. But what is to count as suffering and how is one person's suffering to be weighed against another's? But do difficulties of this sort render the procedural principles of science useless? If not, why should fundamental moral principles be regarded as useless?

Fundamental principles of morality such as fairness and the consideration of interests only give us general criteria of relevance for determining moral issues. They prescribe what sort of considerations are to count as reasons. Within such a framework men have to work out arrangements for organising their lives together. And just as in science there is a fair degree of consensus at a low level of laws, so in the moral case there are basic rules, e.g. concerning contracts, property and the care of the young, which any rational man can see to be necessary to any continuing form of social life, man being what he is and the conditions of life on earth being what they are. For, given that the consideration of interests is a fundamental principle of morality and given that there is room for a vast amount of disagreement about what, ultimately, a man's interest are, there are nevertheless certain general conditions which it is in any man's interest to preserve however idiosyncratic his view of his interests. These include not only the avoidance of pain and injury but also the minimal rules for living together of the type already mentioned. Above this basic level there is room for any amount of disagreement and development. People are too apt to conclude that just because some moral matters are controversial and variable, for instance sexual matters, the whole moral fabric is unstable. It is as if they reason: In Africa men have several wives, in Europe only one, in the U.S.A. only one at a time; therefore all morals are a matter of taste! As evils, murder and theft are just as culture-bound as spitting in the street!

The point surely is that stability and consensus at a basic level are quite compatible with change and experiment at other levels. Indeed to expect any final 'solution', any secure resting place in social or personal life, is to be a victim of the basic illusion which is shared by most opponents of democracy, that of belief in some kind of certainty or perfection. But in determining what are basic rules and in seeking above this level ways of living which may be improvements on those we may have inherited, we make use of principles. Such principles have to be interpreted in terms of concrete traditions; they cannot prescribe precisely what we ought to do, but at least they rule out certain courses of action and sensitise us to features of a situation which are morally relevant. They function more as signposts than as guidebooks.

(c) *The Nature of Principles*

A place for principles in the moral life must therefore be insisted on without making too far-flung claims for what they can prescribe without interpretation by means of a concrete tradition. Indeed I want to insist on the importance of such traditions for the learning of principles as well as for their interpretation. Before, however, this theme is developed in detail, more must be said about the nature of principles in order to remove widespread misunderstandings.

First of all, what are principles? A principle is that which makes a consideration relevant. Suppose that a man is wondering whether gambling is wrong and, in thinking about this, he takes account of the misery caused to the families of gamblers he has known. This shows that he accepts the principle of considering people's interests, for he is sensitised to the suffering caused by gambling rather than horror-struck at the amount of greenness in the world created by the demand for green tables. He does not, in other words, accept the principle of the minimisation of greenness. He may or may not be able to formulate a principle explicitly. But this does not matter; for acceptance of a principle does not depend on the ability to formulate it and to defend it against criticism, as some, like Oakeshott, who are allergic to principles, suggest. Rather it depends on whether a man is sensitised to some considerations and not to others.

Of course, formulation is necessary if one intends to embark on some moral philosophy in the attempt to justify principles. And it might well be said that the task of justifying them is a crucial one for anyone who is according them the importance I am according them. As, however, the central part of my *Ethics and Education* was concerned with this very problem it would be otiose for me to present more than a thumbnail sketch of the arguments here. What I argued was that there are a limited number of principles which are fundamental but non-arbitrary in the sense that they are presuppositions of the form of discourse in which the question 'What are there reasons for doing?' is asked seriously. The principles which have this sort of status are those of impartiality, the consideration of interests, freedom, respect for persons, and probably truth-telling. Such principles are of a procedural sort in that they do not tell us precisely what rules there should be in a society but lay down general guidance about the ways in which we should go about deciding such matters and indicate general criteria of relevance. It was argued that these principles are presuppositions of what is called the democratic way of life, which is based on the conviction that there is a better and a worse way of arranging our social life and that this should be determined by discussion rather than by arbitrary fiat.

Even if it is granted that arguments along these lines might be sustained for a few fundamental principles, further difficulties might still be raised. It might be said, for instance, that stress on the importance of principles in morality implies rigidity in the moral life. A picture is conjured up of Hardy-like characters dourly doing their duty whilst the heavens fall about them. Certainly some kind of firmness is suggested by the phrase 'a man of principle'. But here again, there are misunderstandings. A man of principle is one who is *consistent* in acting in the light of his sensitivity to aspects of a situation that are made morally relevant by a principle. But this does not preclude adaptability due to differences in situations, especially if there is more than one principle which makes different factors in a situation morally important.

Another time-honoured objection is that principles are products of reason and hence inert. We may mouth them or assent to them, but this may be a substitute for acting in a morally appropriate way. Part of the answer to this objection is to be found in the answer to the criticism that links having principles with the ability to formulate them and to defend them. But there is a further point that needs to be made. Notions such as 'fairness' and 'the consideration of interests' are not affectively neutral. 'That is unfair' is an appraisal which has more affinities with an appraisal such as 'that is dangerous' than it has with a colourless judgement such as 'that is oblong'. Pointing out that someone is in pain is not at all like pointing out that he is 5 feet 6 inches tall.

The strength of the emotive theory of ethics derives from the fact that moral principles pick out features of situations which are not affectively neutral. This, however, does not make them inconsistent with living a life guided by reason; for this sort of life presupposes a whole constellation of such appraisals, e.g. that one should be consistent, impartial and truthful, that one should have regard to relevance, accuracy and clarity, and that one should respect evidence and other people as the source of arguments. It is only an irrationalist who welcomes contradictions in an argument, who laughs with delight when accused of inconsistency, or who is nonchalant when convicted of irrelevance. Science and any other rational activity presuppose such normative standards which are intimately connected with the passion for truth which gives point to rational activities. Unless people cared about relevance and had feelings about inconsistency science would not flourish as a form of human life. The usual contrast between reason and feeling is misconceived; for there are attitudes and appraisals which are the passionate side of the life of reason.

So much, then, for the usual objections to the conception of the moral life in which prominence is accorded to principles. I hope I have said enough to establish their place in it. I now want to show how they can be seen to function in relation to concrete traditions to which MacIntyre ascribes so much importance and how they can save us from the existentialist predicament which he views as the logical alternative to being encased in a surviving code.

2 THE COMPLEXITY AND CONCRETENESS OF THE MORAL LIFE

A man who accepts principles is too often represented as living in some kind of social vacuum and attempting to deduce from his principles a concrete way of living. This is an absurd suggestion. To start with, the disposition to appeal to principles is not something that men have by nature, any more than reason itself is some kind of inner gadget that men switch on when the occasion arises. If thinking is the soul's dialogue with itself, the dialogue within mirrors the dialogue without. To be critical is to have kept critical company, to have identified oneself with that segment of society which accepts certain principles in considering its practices. Rationality, of which science is a supreme example, is itself a tradition. Rational men are brought up in the tradition that traditions are not immune from criticism.

But criticism, thinking things out for oneself, and other such activities connected with a rational type of morality, cannot be exercised without some concrete content. For how can one be critical without being brought up in something to be critical of? How can one think things out for oneself unless one's routines break down or one's roles conflict? Adherence to principles must not be conceived of as self-contained; it must be conceived of as being bound up with and modifying some kind of content. Scientists cannot think scientifically without having any content to think about.

(a) *Complexity*
In an open society this content is considerably more complex than in those small, self-contained communities where, according to Mac-Intyre, concepts such as 'good' and 'duty' had their natural home. The notion, for instance, that people are persons with rights and

duties distinct from those connected with their roles is an alien notion in such close-knit communities. But once this is admitted, as was widely the case with the coming of Stoicism and Christianity, the content of the moral life becomes immediately much more complicated. For the norms connected with treating people as persons begin to interpenetrate those connected with roles and with the accepted goals of life. In trying to get a clear idea, therefore, about the contours of our moral life it is necessary to consider its complexity before we can grasp the concrete ways in which principles enter into it. At least five facets of our moral life must be distinguished.

First of all, under concepts such as 'good', 'desirable', and 'worthwhile', fall those activities which are thought to be so important that time must be spent on initiating children into them. These include things such as science, poetry and engineering and possibly a variety of games and pastimes. Most of these are intimately connected not only with occupations and professions but also with possible vocations and ideals of life. In our type of society they provide a variety of options within which an individual can make something of himself if he is encouraged to pursue his own bent as the principle of freedom demands.

Second, under the concepts of 'obligation' and 'duty', fall ways of behaving connected with social roles. Much of a person's moral life is taken up with his station and its duties, with what is required of him as a husband, father, citizen and member of a profession or occupation.

Third, there are those duties, more prominent in an open society, which are not specifically connected with any social role but which relate to the following of general rules governing conduct between members of a society. Rules such as those of unselfishness, fairness and honesty are examples. These affect the manner in which an individual conducts himself within a role as well as in his non-institutionalised relationships with others. They are personalised as character-traits.

Fourth, there are equally wide-ranging goals of life which are personalised in the form of 'motives'. These are purposes not confined to particular activities or roles, which derive from non-neutral appraisals of a man's situation. Examples are ambition, envy, benevolence and greed. An ambitious man, for instance, is one who is moved by the thought of getting ahead of others in a whole variety of contexts. Both traits of character and motives can be thought of as virtues and vices. The traits of fairness and honesty are virtues; those of meanness and selfishness are vices. The motives of benevolence and gratitude are virtues; those of greed and lust are vices. Both character-traits and motives, when looked at in a justificatory context, incorporate considerations that can be regarded as fundamental principles. Examples would be fairness and benevolence, which can be appealed to in order to criticise or justify not only other traits and motives, but also conduct covered by activities and role performances.

There are, finally, very general traits of character which relate not so much to the rules a man follows or to the purposes he pursues as to the manner in which he follows or pursues them. Examples would be integrity, persistence, determination, conscientiousness and consistency. These are all connected with what used to be called 'the will'.

The point in spelling out this complexity of our moral life is to rid us straightaway of any simple-minded view that moral education is just a matter of getting children to have 'good personal relationships' or to observe interpersonal rules like those relating to sex, stealing and selfishness. It emphatically is not. To get a boy committed to some worthwhile activity, such as chemistry or engineering, is no less part of his moral education than damping down his selfishness; so also is getting him really committed to the duties defining his role as a husband or teacher. These duties, of course, must be interpreted in a way which is sensitised by the principle of respect for persons; but no adequate morality could be constituted purely out of free-floating personal obligations.

(b) *Concreteness*

So much for the complexity of the content of the moral life which is to form the basis for any rational morality that appeals to principles. Let me now turn to the matter of concreteness in the interpretation of fundamental principles and moral ideals. The burden of the attack on principles by people like MacIntyre and Winch is to be found in Edmund Burke; it is that they are too abstract. 'The lines of morality are not like the ideal lines of mathematics.' My contention is that principles can be conceived of and must be conceived of as entering into the moral life in a perfectly concrete way without making them completely culture-bound.

Impartiality The most fundamental principle of all practical reasoning is that of impartiality. This is really the demand that excludes arbitrariness, which maintains that distinctions shall be made only where there are relevant differences. This is essential to reasoning, in that what is meant by a reason for doing A rather than B is some aspect under which it is viewed which makes it relevantly different. But though this principle gives negative guidance in that it rules out arbitrariness, making an exception of oneself, and so on, it is immediately obvious that it is quite impossible to apply without some other principle which determines criteria of relevance. The most obvious principle to supply such criteria is that of the consideration of interests, which is personalised in virtues such as benevolence and kindness.

The Consideration of Interests   In practice the rays of this principle are largely refracted through the prism of our social roles and general duties as members of a society. If we are teachers, for instance, considering people's interests amounts, to a large extent, to considering the interests of children entrusted to our care. I once taught with a man who had such a wide-ranging concern for people's interests that he used to tell his class to get on with some work and to sit there with them, writing letters to old scholars, in order to get them to subscribe to an 'Aid to India' fund. His present scholars were, of course, bored to death! He certainly had a somewhat abstract approach to considering people's interests!

Most Utilitarians, following Mill and Sidgwick, have stressed the importance of Mill's 'secondary principles' in morality. The Utilitarian, Mill argued, has not got to be constantly weighing the effects of his actions on people's interests any more than a Christian has to read through the Bible every time before he acts. The experience of a society with regard to the tendencies of actions in relation to people's interests lies behind its roles and general rules. The principle that one should consider people's interests acts also as an ever-present corrective to, and possible ground of criticism of, rules and social practices which can also be appealed to when rules conflict. This point is well made by Stephen Toulmin in his book on ethics. A man could stick too closely to his role and accept too uncritically what was expected of him generally as a member of society. He might be very much an organisation man or a man of puritanical disposition, riddled with rules that might have lost their point, or without sensitivity to the suffering caused by unthinking insistence on the letter of the law. What would be lacking would be that sensitivity to suffering caused by actions and social practices which finds expression in virtues such as benevolence, kindness and what Hume called 'the sentiment of humanity'.

Freedom Giving interpersonal support to the consideration of interests. is the principle of freedom which lays it down that, other things being equal, people should be allowed to do what they want, or that, in other words, reasons should be given for constraining people in their pursuit of what they take to be good. This combines two notions, that of 'wants' and that of 'constraints', and immediately the concrete questions crowd in 'What is it that people might want to do?' and 'What sorts of constraints should be absent?' What, too, is to count as a constraint? Is it the want to walk about nude or to speak one's mind in public that is at issue? And are the constraints those of the bully or those of public opinion? The situation becomes even more complicated once we realise that, men being what they are, we are only in fact free from obnoxious constraints like those of the bully if we are willing to accept the milder and more levelling constraints of law. And so concreteness asserts itself. The principle only provides a general presumption, albeit one of far-reaching importance. At what point we decide that there are good reasons for constraining people because, for instance, they are damaging the interests of others, is a matter of judgement.

Closely related to the principle of freedom are ideals like 'the self-development of the individual' and personal autonomy. But here again, concreteness is imperative, for what can 'development' mean unless we build into the concept those modes of experience that it has taken the human race so long to evolve? And what sort of 'self' is going to develop? Granted that this must come to a certain extent from the individual, who does this partly by his 'choices', must not this 'self' be fairly closely related to the normal stock of motives and character-traits which are called virtues? And is it not desirable that higher-order character-traits, such as persistence and integrity, be exhibited in the development of this 'self'? And how can the pressure for independence and the making of choices arise unless the individual genuinely feels conflicting obligations deriving from his occupancy of social roles and his acceptance of the general rules of a society? And what point is there in choice unless the individual thinks that what he decides can be better or worse, wise or foolish? And if he thinks that any particular act is not a pointless performance he must already accept that there are general principles which pick out relevant features of the alternatives open to him.

All of this adds up to the general conclusion that the ideals connected with the principle of freedom are unintelligible except against a background of desirable activities, roles and rules between which the individual has to choose and that any proper choice (as distinct from random plumping) presupposes principles other than freedom in the light of which alternatives can be assessed.

Respect for Persons   The same sort of point can be made about respect for persons, another fundamental principle which underlies and acts as a corrective to so many of our formalised dealings with other men. Indeed, much of the content of this principle has to be defined negatively in such concrete contexts. To show lack of respect for a person is, for instance, to treat him in a role situation as merely a functionary, to be impervious to the fact that he, like us, has aspirations that matter to him, is a centre of evaluation and choice, takes pride in his achievements, and has his own unique point of view on the world. Or it is to treat him merely as a participant in an activity who is to be assessed purely in terms of his skill and competence in that activity. Worse at something becomes generalised to worse as a human being. In a similar way an excess of group loyalty or fellow-feeling can make a man seem not just different in some respects but generally inferior as a human being. Respect for persons, too, is at the bottom of our conviction that some motives are vices – lust, for instance, and envy and a certain kind of humility.

So much, then, by way of a brief sketch to illustrate the way in which I conceive of fundamental principles as entering into the moral life in a manner perfectly consistent with its complexity and concreteness. I now want to end by outlining my conception of moral education, which goes with this conception of the moral life.

3 MORAL EDUCATION

One or two general remarks must first be made about the meaning of 'education'. There is a well-established generalised use of 'education' which refers, roughly, to any processes of 'rearing', 'instruction', 'training', etc., that go on at home and at school. But there is a more specific sense of education which emerged in the nineteenth century in which education is distinguished from training and which is used to pick out processes that lead to the development of an 'educated man'. In this more specific sense, education involves getting people to make something of themselves within activities that are thought to be worthwhile, in a way which involves an understanding that has some kind of depth and breadth to it. In this more specific sense of education, employed by most educators when they are thinking about their tasks, all education is, therefore, moral education, if we are to include the pursuit of good in morals and not just confine it to codes and more general dealings with other men. Again, we will have to leave on one side the vexatious question of justification in the sphere of 'the good', of why, in other words, chemistry is more worthwhile than baseball or sun-bathing. We can pursue the implications of this view of education without getting immersed in that issue, which is a veritable 'Serbonian bog where armies whole have sunk'.

The first implication is that educating people has very much to do with getting them 'on the inside' of what is worthwhile, so that they come to pursue and appreciate it for what there is in it as distinct from what they may conceive of it as leading on to. It is in relation to this criterion of education that I want to make sense of notions such as commitment and being authentic, which starkly confront the instrumental attitude of 'What is the use of it?' and 'Where is this going to get one?' I have sympathy for the philosopher who was pressed at an interview for a chair to commit himself to the view that philosophy must have some practical use – whatever that means. He exclaimed in exasperation: 'Look, we may have to say that sort of thing in order to get money from governments and businessmen for universities, but for heaven's sake do not let us become victims of our own propaganda.'

The second implication is that educating people must involve knowledge and understanding. To be educated is not just to have mastered a know-how or knack, even if it is in the sphere of some very worthwhile activity such as cookery or ballet dancing. The Spartans were highly trained and skilled, but they are almost paradigms of a people who were not educated. Though depth of understanding is necessary to being educated, it is not sufficient, for a scientist can have a deep understanding of the 'reasons why' of things and still be uneducated if all he understands is a specialised branch of science. 'Education is of the whole man' is a conceptual truth in that being educated is inconsistent with being only partially developed in one's understanding – with seeing a car, for instance, as only a piece of machinery without aesthetic grace, without a history and without potentialities for human good or ill. Let me now relate these two implications to the different facets of the moral life in order to show the indispensability of both content and principles and the proper place for the romantic ideal.

(a) *Commitment and Authenticity*
One of the great enemies of education, in this specific sense, is second-handedness and instrumentality; hence Whitehead's polemic against inert ideas. What seems deplorable is not just that children should

mug up some science because it is the done thing or in order to get good grades but that teachers should grind through their day with that dreadful fixed smile, or that people should be polite without sensing the point of it. Doing the done thing for conformity's sake seems a stifling corruption of the moral life, and it is inherently unstable outside a confined context; for a second-hand form of behaviour is very susceptible to temptations and disintegrates when external pressures and incentives are withdrawn. This is tantamount to saying that moral education is centrally concerned with the development of certain types of motives, especially with what I have called the rational passions. When looked at in a justificatory context, some of these, e.g. benevolence, respect for persons and the sense of justice, function as fundamental principles. But if such principles are to be operative in a person's conduct, they must become *his* principles. That means that they must come to function as motives, as considerations of a far-ranging sort that actually move him to act. Let us now consider the different facets of the moral life in the light of this commitment criterion of education.

Activities and Role-performances The trouble with the situation in which we are placed in education is not just that children do not always come to us glistening with a desire to learn what is worthwhile or with a predisposition toward mastering their duties; it is also that they are incapable of first-hand attitudes toward these activities and role performances until they are sufficiently on the inside of them to grasp them and be committed to what they involve. Although a child may have some degree of curiosity there is a great difference between this and the passion for truth which lies at the heart of an activity such as science, and until he feels strongly about this all-pervading principle that permeates science, it is difficult to see how his viewpoint can be anything but a bit external. He must, to a certain extent, be induced to go through the motions before he is in a position to grasp their point, and the point is given by the underlying principle, which personalises one of the rational passions. To be rational is to care about truth; similarly, in the interpersonal sphere he must come to care about persons as centres of evaluation.

Of course there are all sorts of devices for bringing this about. In the old days, teachers, modelling the school on the army, used to employ a variety of coercive techniques. The progressives, in revolt, model the school more on the supermarket and try to gear their wares to children's wants and preferences. Then there are the less dramatic devices of stimulating by example and employing general guiding words such as 'good' and 'ought', which suggest that there are reasons but do not intimate clearly what the reasons are. The teacher's hope is that the proper reasons for doing things will become the pupil's actual reasons. This may come about by some process of identification. Admiration for a teacher may be turned outward toward involvement in the activities and forms of behaviour to which he is committed, or an existing predisposition in the child, such as curiosity, may be gradually transformed by appropriate experience into the rational passion of respect for truth. This is likely to be greatly facilitated if the enthusiasm of the peer group is also enlisted, but this takes time and training. Let me illustrate this.

To be on the inside of an activity such as science or philosophy is not to have just a general curiosity or a merely abstract concern for truth. It is to be concretely concerned about whether particular points of view are true or false. These particularities are only intelligible within a continuing tradition of thought, which has been developed by people who adhere to a public stock of procedural principles. It is because of this concrete concern that they care desperately about things like the relevance of remarks, cogency in argument and clarity of exposition; for how can one get to the bottom of anything without a concern about standards such as these which are indispensable to serious discussion? Sporadic curiosity is not enough; it has to be fanned into a steady flame and disciplined by adherence to the standards which regulate a common pursuit. The problem of education, as Whitehead saw only too well, is not just that of contriving the initial romance, it is that of bringing about acceptance of the precision and discipline required to wed a person to a pursuit. In this the support of the peer group is probably as important as the example and insistence of the teacher.

The judgement and skill which come with first-hand experience render activities more absorbing and worthwhile. The cultivation of personal relationships, for instance, and even sitting on committees, can become more and more absorbing as occupations for those who have a shrewd grasp of human behaviour. Politics, as an activity, was quite different when practised by Caesar rather than by Pompey, because of the skill and understanding Caesar brought to it. Although it is satisfying sometimes to relapse into routine activities requiring little effort (a point, I think, which Dewey appreciated too little), and although there is something to be said for occasional incursions into simple, and sometimes more brutish forms of enjoyment, it would be intolerable for a rational man to spend most of his life in such a circumscribed way. A minimum task of moral education is surely to equip people so that they will not be perpetually bored. Therefore, the case for skill and understanding, on grounds purely of individual satisfaction, is a strong one. There is also the point that, as soon as knowledge enters in as an important ingredient in an activity, an additional dimension of value, deriving from the concern for truth, is opened up.

In a pluralistic society like ours there must be a high degree of consensus at the level of those fundamental principles which underlie democratic procedures and, as I have already argued, it is obvious enough that there must be agreement about a level of basic rules which provide conditions necessary for anyone to pursue his interests. But above this level there is bound to be controversy. In this sphere of 'the good' or of personal ideals, with which we are at the moment concerned, there are any number of options open to individuals. And the principle of freedom demands that there should be. It is in this sphere that talk of commitment and authenticity is particularly pertinent. One man may develop a lifelong passion for science. Another, more influenced by the Christian ideal, may find that his main sphere of commitment is in the sphere of personal relationships and the relief of suffering. Another may opt for an aesthetic type of activity.

On the other hand, another person may find almost complete fulfilment in devoting himself to the fulfilment of a role, that of a teacher for instance. There has been a lot of loose talk, deriving from Sartre's celebrated example of the waiter, about the incompatibility of authenticity with occupying a role. Playing a role, which involves either simulation or second-handedness, should not be confused with a genuine commitment to a role. And, of course, as has been emphasised repeatedly, there is no role which can *completely* contain one's concerns and duties as a human being.

Interpersonal Rules　In the interpersonal sphere there may have to be firm insistence from the start on rules like those of keeping contracts, not stealing, punctuality and honesty. And why should children not *enjoy* mastering these rules as well as those of games? Unless, however, the reasons behind these rules eventually become the individual's reasons, the job is only half done. And this does not mean fostering a theoretical grasp of the conduciveness of such rules to the general good. That kind of notion never induced anyone to do anything except to preach theoretical revolution. Neither does it mean being swept by occasional gusts of sympathy when it dawns that somebody has suffered because he has been let down. It means, on the contrary, a steady but intense sensitivity to the consequences of actions, a constant and imaginative realisation that in interpersonal relations one is dealing with persons who also have their unique point of view on the world and that this is something about them which matters supremely. In other words, it means the development of motives which personalise fundamental principles. It means also the development of judgement about particular moral matters that can only come to a person who has really got on the inside of this mode of experience. Making decisions and choices is too often represented as agonising. For those who have attained some degree of wisdom it can be both a challenge and a delight.

It is not for a philosopher to pronounce on how children can be got on the inside of this more rational form of life, or on how the rational passions, which personalise fundamental principles, can best be awakened and developed. That is a matter for psychologists. The philosopher's role is only to indicate the sort of job that has to be done. But what he *can* say is that all talk of commitment and being authentic is vacuous unless this sort of job *is* done; for it is pointless to mouth these general injunctions unless concrete provision is made to implement them. What is to be lamented about young people today is not their lack of idealism but the difficulty of harnessing it to concrete tasks. Demonstrations, like mourning, are often symbolic expressions of feelings that have no obvious channel of discharge in appropriate action.

The Will   The importance of the rational passions can also be shown in the sphere of what used to be called 'the will', where notions like those of integrity, determination and resoluteness have their place. Of course this form of consistency is possible for people who adhere conscientiously to a simple code, perhaps because, like the colonel in *The Bridge on the River Kwai*, they accept unthinkingly some role-regulating principle such as 'one ought always to obey orders' or 'an officer must always care for his men'. But such consistency is also possible for people with a more complicated morality if they genuinely care about the considerations which are incorporated in fundamental principles. Strength of character is so often represented in negative terms as saying no to temptation, as standing firm, as being impervious to social pressure. My guess is that rational people are able to do this only if they are passionately devoted to fairness, freedom and the pursuit of truth, and if they have a genuine respect for others and are intensely concerned if they suffer. The rational passion for consistency itself is also an important positive type of motivation. Indeed it has an all-pervasive influence on a rational person's beliefs and conduct. So much, then, for the first aspect of education, which concerns commitment to what is worthwhile. I now pass briefly to the second: that concerned with depth and breadth of understanding.

(b) *Depth and Breadth of Understanding*

In any worthwhile activity or form of behaviour there is a mode of acting or thinking, with its underlying principles, and some kind of established content which incorporates the experience of those who are skilled in this sphere. Depth is provided partly by the principles immanent in the mode of experience and partly by the degree to which it has been possible to discern the one in the many in the content.

The sin, of course, of the old formalism was to hand on content in a second-hand way without encouraging children to get on the inside of activities and to master the appropriate mode of experience for themselves. The converse sin of the progressive was to imagine that children could go it alone without any proper grasp of content or of the underlying mode of experience with its immanent principles. A more modern sin is to assume that a mode of experience, or a methodology, can be formalised and handed out and children saved the trouble of mastering any content. Don't bother, it is said, to teach children any historical facts, just teach them to think histori-cally. This reminds me of the yearning, which one so often encoun-ters, that one should hand out rules for Clear Thinking in twelve easy lessons or that one should set out philosophical method in advance of dealing with particular philosophical arguments. Enough, I hope, has been said about the intimate relationship between principles and concrete content to avoid that particular rationalistic delusion.

In the interpersonal sphere of morality there is, of course, a basic content, which every child must master, of rules to do with non-injury, property, contracts and so on; but depth of understanding in this sphere is rather different. It is not like depth of understanding in the sciences, which consists in grasping more and more abstract theories; for in morality one comes very quickly to non-arbitrary stopping points in fundamental principles, such as the consideration of interests. Depth consists rather in the development of the imagina-tion so that one can become more acutely aware of content to be given to these principles. What, for instance, is a man's interest? Above the level of physical and mental health what is to count? Surely not just what he thinks his interest to be? And so we start trying to understand various forms of worthwhile activity and personal ideals, not only in general but in relation to the capacity of particular individuals.

Respect for persons also opens up endless vistas for the imagination in making us vividly aware of the extent to which we drag our feet in failing to treat individuals and classes of people as persons in a full sense. It opens up, too, the whole realm of our understanding of persons. For understanding a person is more than being able to interpret his behaviour in terms of wide-ranging psychological generalisations – even if there were any such generalisations that had been established – and it is not a mystic confrontation of 'I' with 'thou', about which there is little coherent that can be said. It is something about which a great deal can be said which is of cardinal importance for the moral life – about the way in which an individual's outlook is shaped by his roles, about his traits and about his motives and aspirations. But most of this sort of knowledge we obtain by being with a person and sharing a common life with him, not by delving in psychological textbooks. This sort of knowledge is probably the most important sort for any moral agent to have; for our detailed appraisals of people are very closely intertwined with explanatory notions. Indeed, I made the point earlier that most motives and traits are also virtues or vices. And it may take a whole novel such as *Howards End* to explore concretely the range of an emotion like indignation.

Breadth of understanding, however, is of equal importance to depth in any concrete approach to the moral life. It has been argued that this life itself is a complex affair involving roles, activities, motives and interpersonal rules. It also involves the disposition to be critical of this wide-ranging content in which any generation must necessarily be nurtured. The individual, too, may be confronted with conflicts arising from this heritage. How is he to be critical in an intelligent way about a social practice or about a particular feature of government policy unless he has some understanding of history and of the sorts of facts and unintended consequences of actions with which the social sciences are concerned? How is he to choose realistically between alternatives open to him unless he knows some facts?

It is absurd to encourage children to be critical and autonomous and not to insist on them learning facts which may inform their criticism and choices. In England, at the moment, we have all sorts of variants on the topic-centred curriculum, which is meant to induce moral commitment and to sensitise children to social issues. Discussion, of course, is the thing; it is regarded as almost sinful nowadays to instruct children in anything! But too often all that such discussions achieve is to confirm people's existing prejudices. They are not used as launching pads to dispatch children to the realm of some hard facts in the light of which they might make up their minds in an informed manner.

The same sort of point can be made about the necessity of breadth if children are to choose for themselves the sphere of activity within the wide range of what is desirable, to which they are to become personally committed and which may form the nucleus of a personal ideal. Not only must they have some breadth of content in order to be provided with concrete samples of the sorts of things between which they must choose; they must also make a concrete study of some of the forms of experience which have a special position in informing their choice. By this I mean studies such as literature, history, religion and the social sciences, which, if imaginatively entered into, enlarge one's perspective of the predicament of man and so put one's own choice in a less abstract setting. The romantic ideal must at least have a classical background, if it is to function as more than a mere protest.

CONCLUSION

It might be said that my conception of moral education is indistinguishable from the ideal of a liberal education. I do not mind putting it this way provided that 'liberal' implies no wishy-washiness and is used with awareness of the distinct emphases that it intimates.

A liberal education, to start with, is one that stresses the pursuit of what is worthwhile for what is intrinsic to it. It is hostile to a purely instrumental view of activities, to the bonds that link whatever is done to some palpable extrinsic end. The moral life, I have argued, rests upon rational passions which permeate a whole range of activities and which make them worthwhile for their own sake.

A liberal education is secondly one that is not narrowly confined to particular perspectives. I have argued both for a broad interpretation of the moral life and for the necessity of breadth of understanding to give concrete backing to the ideal of freedom, which is the most obvious ideal of liberalism.

Thirdly, a liberal education is one that is incompatible with authoritarianism and dogmatism. This is because a liberal education is based ultimately on respect for truth which depends on reasons and not on the word or will of any man, body or book. This means, of course, not that there is not an important place for authority in social life, but that it has to be rationally justified – as indeed it can be in the bringing up of children. The use of authority must not be confused with authoritarianism. Respect for truth is intimately connected with fairness and respect for persons, which, together with freedom, are fundamental principles which underlie our moral life and which are personalised in the form of the rational passions. The central purpose, however, of my essay, has been to show that adherence to such principles is a passionate business and that they can and should enter in a very concrete way into a man's activities, roles and more personal dealings with other men.

Chapter 5

Moral Development:
A Plea for Pluralism*

INTRODUCTION

Much of moral philosophy in the past has been unconvincing because
it has not dwelt sufficiently on the different views that can be taken
about what is morally important. It has been bedevilled by monistic
theories such as Utilitarianism, or some version of Kant's theory, in
which the attempt is made to demonstrate that one type of justification can be given for everything which there are reasons for doing or
being. Keeping promises, telling the truth, the pursuit of poetry
rather than of push-pin, being courageous and being just have all
been fitted into a monolithic mould provided by some fundamental
principle. The result has been an artificial type of theory that has
never quite rung true. Utilitarians, for instance, who have usually
been decent people with developed moral sensitivities, have invented
highly dubious, and quite untested empirical speculations to demonstrate that their conviction that they should be just and truthful,
which would never really dream of giving up, rests on alleged consequences to human welfare.

There is a danger of a similar fate befalling theories of moral
development. It may well be that some generalisations have been
established about certain aspects of moral development; but these
may be peculiar to the limited range of phenomena studied. It would
be unfortunate if these generalisations were erected into a general

* My thanks are due to the Australian National University for the facilities
provided for me as a Visiting Fellow which enabled me to write this article, and to
Geoffrey Mortimore of the Philosophy Department of A.N.U., whose thesis on
Virtue and Vice put me on the track of some important differences between
virtues, and whose comments helped me to revise a first draft of this article.

theory of moral development without account being taken of the differences exhibited by the phenomena that have not been studied.

In developing this thesis I shall use Kohlberg's cognitive stage theory as my point of departure; for his work in this field seems to me to be by far the most important which has been done to date. Yet I have certain doubts about it. Some of these derive from his failure to spell out certain points in more detail; others derive from the thought that there is much more to morality than is covered by his theory, and that his generalisations may be true only of the area of morality on which he has concentrated his attention. My article will be divided, therefore, into five main parts: exposition of Kohlberg's theory; some doubts about details; virtues and habits; is Kohlberg prescribing a morality?; and Freud and moral failure.

1 EXPOSITION OF KOHLBERG'S THEORY

Kohlberg claims, like Piaget, that there are invariant sequences in development which hold in any culture. He produces evidence to show, for instance, that in any culture children begin by being unable to distinguish dreams from real events. They then grasp that dreams are not real; then that they cannot be seen by others, and take place inside the dreamer; then that they are immaterial events produced by the dreamer, like thoughts (Kohlberg, 1968b, pp. 1024–9). He makes two points about this sequence which, he claims, hold for all proper developmental sequences. First, he claims that this sequence could not have a different order. It depends upon the relationships of concepts such as 'unreal', 'internal', 'immaterial', which it would take too long to explicate. Secondly, he claims that this sequence cannot be fully explained in terms of the teaching of adults; for if adults taught anything about dreams, they would tend to use concepts about them appropriate to a much later stage, which would not explain how children go through the earlier stages. Also, the same sequence can be observed in cultures where adults have different beliefs about dreams.

Piaget has, of course, extensively illustrated this thesis about invariant order depending upon relationships between concepts in the case of mathematics and elementary physics, and, to a more limited extent, in the moral sphere, where Kohlberg has elaborated this thesis. He holds that, though there is a difference between cultures in the *content* of moral beliefs, the development of their *form* is a cultural invariant. In other words, though there is variation between cultures about whether or not people should, for example, be thrifty or have sexual relationships outside marriage, there are cross-cultural uniformities relating to how such rules are conceived – for example, as ways of avoiding punishment, as laid down by authority. Children, Kohlberg claims, start by seeing rules as dependent upon power and external compulsion; they then see them as instrumental to rewards and to the satisfaction of their needs; then as ways of obtaining social approval and esteem; then as upholding some ideal order; and finally as articulations of social principles necessary to living together with others – especially, justice. Varying contents given to rules are fitted into invariant forms of conceiving rules. Of course, in many cultures there is no progression through to the final stages, the rate of development will vary in different cultures, and in the same culture there are great individual differences. All this can be granted and explained. But Kohlberg's main point is that this sequence in levels of conceiving rules is constitutive of moral development and that it is a cultural invariant.

How, then, does Kohlberg think that this type of development occurs if it is not the result of teaching? He rejects maturation theories as non-starters except in the case of abilities such as walking. He also rejects three types of socialisation hypotheses. First, he claims that a whole mass of empirical studies have failed to confirm the findings of the psycho-analytic school. There are no correlations, for instance, between parental modes of handling infantile drives and later moral behaviour and attitudes. There are no correlations between the amount of reward given and moral variables. Findings on parental attitudes give no clear support for the theory that early identifications are central to a moral orientation. The only established correlation, he claims, is between what he calls 'induction', which often goes along with the withdrawal of love, and moral guilt. By 'induction' he means cognitive stimulation connected with the awareness of the consequences of actions. Similarly, there is a correlation between maternal warmth and the development of conscience. But this operates, he maintains, by providing only a climate for learning (Kohlberg, 1964).

Secondly, he maintains that the evidence from the classic Hartshorne–May study shows overwhelmingly that the theory of habit generalisation put forward by psychologists with a learning theory type of orientation has no validity. What came out of this mammoth enquiry was that the traits such as honesty are situation-specific. Moral learning of this sort can only bring about specific forms of behaviour conformity. It cannot bring about predictable behaviour over a wide range of situations, such as is found in a person who has emerged to the principled stage of morality. He also claims that learning theorists have produced no evidence whatever about the influence of early forms of habit training on later adult behaviour.

Thirdly, Kohlberg rejects Piaget's hypothesis, which he got from Durkheim, that the peer-group plays a decisive role in moral development in the sense that its norms are internalised by the individual. There is a correlation between the development of a principled morality and peer-group participation. But Kohlberg argues that this is because of the stimulation which such a group provides for the individual to reflect upon situations (Kohlberg, 1968a).

How then does Kohlberg think that these Kantian categories, which provide forms of conceiving of rules at the different stages, evolve? He rejects Kant's own view that they are innate moulds into which specific experiences are fitted (Kohlberg, 1968b, p. 1023). He argues that they develop as a result of interaction between the child and his physical and social environment. To understand how this happens it is necessary, therefore, to analyse, first, the universal structural features of the environment; secondly, the logical relationships involved between the concepts; and thirdly, the relationship between the particular child's conceptual scheme and the type of experience with which he is confronted. In order for development to take place there must be an optimal amount of discrepancy between the two.

This interactionist theory of development is applied to the moral sphere. Kohlberg thinks that the stages of development represent culturally invariant sequences in the child's conception of himself and his social world.

'It implies, then, that there are some universal structural dimensions in the social world, as there are in the physical world. . . . These dimensions are universal because the basic structure of social and moral action is the universal structure provided by the existence of a self in a world composed of other selves who are both like the self and different from it' (Kohlberg, unpublished manuscript).

He follows Baldwin and Mead in ascribing great importance to role taking and the dawning of reciprocity in the development of this understanding of the social situation in which we are placed. Social and moral understanding develop *pari passu* with other forms of cognitive development. And just as contact with the physical world gradually stimulates the child, for example, to classify it in terms of objects having causal relationships with others, so also in the social and moral case, the child is led gradually to grasp principles which must obtain if individuals are to live together and to satisfy their claims as social beings who are both similar to and different from others.

In support of his thesis, Kohlberg claims that the main factors which have been shown to correlate with the development of a principled, predictable morality are intelligence, moral knowledge (that is, knowledge of the rules of a society), the tendency to anticipate future events, the ability to maintain focused attention, the capacity to control unsocialised fantasies, and self-esteem. The major consistencies in moral conduct represent decision-making capacities rather than fixed behaviour traits (Kohlberg, 1964).

It is difficult to know where to begin in criticising a theory which is so varied in its claims, but an obvious strategy which matches Kohlberg's manner of presentation suggests itself. Questions can first be asked about the acceptability of his positive theory. Then, as he puts this forward as an alternative to theories which stress habit formation and to Freudian theory, questions can be raised about his grounds for dismissing theories of this sort. It might well be, for instance, that if morality is not as unitary an affair as he suggests, there is some place for habit formation in some of the areas of morality which he rather disregards. Similarly, he assumes that Freud was trying to answer the same sorts of questions about moral development as those on which he and Piaget have concentrated. But if Freud was in fact concerned with a different range of questions, then Kohlberg's criticisms of Freud might not be altogether apposite. This is the strategy which I will, in fact, use in commenting upon Kohlberg's theories. Doubts will first be raised about some of the details of his positive theory; doubts will then be raised about his dismissal of other theories in the field; and these doubts derive from the thought that Kohlberg adopts too simple and too monolithic an approach to moral development.

2 SOME DOUBTS ABOUT DETAILS

If Kohlberg's cross-cultural claims are confirmed, they are the most important findings in the psychology of morals since those of Piaget, which have often been criticised for being culture-bound. Most people, on reflection, would be prepared to concede that there is some kind of culturally invariant order of development in the case of mathematical or scientific forms of experience; but they would regard morality as much more relative to culture both in its form and in its content. Nevertheless, leaving aside the validity of the empirical findings, there are some conceptual difficulties about Kohlberg's account which could, perhaps, be dispelled if he were to spell out in more detail what he has in mind.

Let us start by probing into what he claims to be the two main features of all proper developmental sequences as applied to this particular case, namely that the order of conceptual development could not be otherwise for logical reasons and that development does not depend upon teaching.

(a) *Order of Development and Logical Relations between Concepts*
In his account of stages of moral development, Kohlberg has, for a variety of reasons, elaborated Piaget's three stages of egocentric, transcendental and autonomous morality into six stages by making a sub-division within each stage. The egocentric stage, for instance, is subdivided into the stage when rules are seen as dependent upon power and external compulsion, and the stage when they are seen as instrumental to rewards and to the satisfaction of the child's needs. He claims that this order of stages could not be otherwise than it is because of the logical relationships between the concepts. What can this mean in this particular case? In a general way the claim might seem to hold of Piaget's three stages. For instance, it is difficult to see how an autonomous morality could come before a transcendental one, for an autonomous morality implies that one can raise questions about the validity of rules and accept or reject them after reflection. Unless, therefore, one already has been introduced in some way to rules and knows, from the inside, what it is to follow a rule, there would be no content in relation to which one could exercise one's autonomy. But surely a similar point cannot be made so easily about connecting rules with power and external compulsion as distinct from connecting them with rewards and with the satisfaction of needs. It may be empirically true that children do conceive of rules in these different ways in this order. But what is there in the concepts concerned which might convert this discovered order into some kind of logical order? That there must be some explanation of this sort seems a reasonable hypothesis; how else could the culturally invariant order be explained? For instance, one might plausibly suggest that the conceptual structure required for seeing rules as means to getting rewards must be more sophisticated than that required merely for seeing them as ways of avoiding things that are unpleasant. Children have, for instance, to have a more determinate

conception of the future; they have to be able to conceive of things as positively pleasant, rather than as things which either hurt or ease an unpleasant condition of need. As a matter of empirical fact, their behaviour can be influenced by external compulsion and interference much sooner than it can be influenced by offering them rewards, and it could be shown that this is no accident, because of the conceptual structure required to see things as rewards. A similar analysis could probably be given of why seeing rules as connected with rewards must come before seeing them as connected with approval, for, conceptually speaking, 'approval' is a much more sophisticated notion than 'reward'. I have no doubt that some detailed work on the concepts concerned could reveal the kind of connections that have to be revealed. Kohlberg links these stages of moral development with a theory of role-taking and with more general features of a child's developing understanding of other people in relationship to himself. It may well be that he can, by means of this type of analysis, make it intelligible why the child *must* conceive of rules in the order in which they in fact conceive of them. But it is incumbent on Kohlberg to spell out these connections explicitly at every point. Otherwise his theory fails to carry conviction; for it does not manifestly satisfy one of the two main conditions which, on his own view, a proper developmental theory must satisfy, namely, that the temporal order of the stages should reflect some kind of logical order in the forms of conception characterising each of the stages.

(b) *Teaching and Moral Development*

The second condition which a proper developmental theory must satisfy is that the progression from stage to stage is not brought about by the teaching of adults. Kohlberg claims that the transition from one level of understanding to another can be aided by cognitive stimulation which helps to establish an optimal amount of discrepancy between what the child has already mastered and what he has yet to master. But this cannot be brought about by explicit teaching.

This seems, at first, to be rather a startling point which has a counter-intuitive thrust to it, to put it mildly. Surely Kohlberg cannot mean, it might be said, that saying things to children such as 'That's not fair' plays no part in helping them to develop the concept of 'fairness'. How could children ever learn such a complicated concept unless the word was used by someone in situations in which the concept had application? It is difficult to be sure what Kohlberg is asserting because he gives no account of what he means either by 'teaching' or by 'cognitive stimulation', with which he contrasts teaching. He suggests that much of the *content* of morality is passed on by example and instruction, but the *form* is something which the individual has to come to understand for himself with appropriate stimulation from others and from typical concrete situations. This, he claims, provides the appropriate psychological rationale for Socrates' conception of education, in which the learner is gradually brought to see things for himself – not haphazardly, but in a tightly structured situation (Kohlberg, 1970).

In making this sort of contrast, Kohlberg surely displays an over-rigid conception of what teaching is. Socrates was teaching the slave all right even though he was not telling him things. He was asking him leading questions, getting him to concentrate on some things rather than on others, putting questions in sequences so that the slave came gradually to make certain crucial connections. 'Teaching' surely can be applied to a great variety of processes which have in common the feature that something is marked out, displayed, made plain so that someone can learn. Information, skills and attitudes are taught in different ways. But, if they are taught, there is always some process by means of which attention is drawn to the different types of things that have to be mastered. In the case of the learning of principles, which is what Kohlberg is talking about, this marking out can also be present. But it can only take the learner a certain way. If information which has to be memorised is being imparted, the teacher can instruct the learner explicitly in what has to be learned; in teaching a skill the particular movement can be demonstrated explicitly for the learner to copy and practise. But when what is being taught is a principle which provides some kind of unity to a whole number of previously disconnected items, the teacher can only put the matter this way and that until the learner comes to 'see' it or understand it. If, therefore, the teacher is trying to get the child to 'see' something that is characteristic of one of the developmental stages, all he can do is to draw attention to common features of cases and hope that the penny will drop. He cannot get him to memorise some explicit content, or practice some movement, as in the case of imparting information or training in a skill.

There is another feature, too, of this kind of learning which makes the notion of *specific* teaching inapplicable. A child may be brought to grasp a principle by being confronted, in a variety of ways, with particular examples. But once, as Wittgenstein put it, he knows how to go on, there is no limit to the number of cases that he will see as falling under this principle. There is a sense, therefore in this sort of learning, in which the learner gets out much more than anyone could possibly have put in. Kohlberg's objection to *specific* teaching is therefore readily explained; for, in this sense, principles just are not the sorts of things that can be regarded as applying to only a specific number of items which could be imparted by a teacher.

It looks, therefore, as if Kohlberg's thesis about the impossibility of adults bringing about conceptual development by teaching is either false or a conceptual truth. It is false if a normal, non-restrictive concept of 'teaching' is being employed; for it is manifestly the case that children's understanding can be accelerated by a variety of processes such as presenting them with examples and so on. Kohlberg may call this 'cognitive stimulation'; but most people would call it 'teaching'. It is a conceptual truth if a restricted concept of 'teaching' is being employed, which rules out the processes by means of which adults help to get the child into a position where he can grasp a principle. Understanding a principle is just not the sort of thing that can be imparted by instruction, example, training and other such processes.

There is a further point, perhaps, about the actual effectiveness of leaving the child alone to make his own connections, as distinct from trying to lead him to the brink as Socrates did with the slave. My guess is that what one says about this will depend very much on the types of principles that are being learnt. If one takes, for instance, the forms of conception that are features of the different developmental stages, it is not obvious what can be done about these – for example, coming to see a rule as connected with approval rather than with rewards. Kohlberg, however, like Piaget, regards other principles as of equal developmental importance – for example, that actions should be assessed in terms of their intentions rather than in terms of their objective consequences, as in the case of the child who thinks that what is crucial about breaking cups is whether the breaker intended it, as distinct from the number of cups that are in fact broken. In a sense, both these are 'formal' notions, but in very different ways, and it could be that the teaching of adults, in the non-restrictive sense of 'teaching', could play a larger part in helping children to grasp the latter principle than the former.

Kohlberg's thesis about the learning of principles, however, though it looks like some kind of conceptual truth about learning, is a very important one to emphasise at a time when there is much pointless controversy between those who emphasise 'activity' and 'discovery' methods and those who emphasise more traditional methods of instruction and training. The general point must first be made that the method used is limited severely by what it is that has to be learnt. Discovery methods have little application to the learning of skills or to the acquiring of information. However, in so far as there are principles which have to be understood in the type of learning that is taking place, the sorts of methods included by Kohlberg under 'cognitive stimulation' have manifest application. They also apply to the grasping of those principles – for example, of causality or of the relevance of intended consequences in morality – which constitute *one* type of what Kohlberg calls the 'form' of experience. Instruction, training and learning by example seem much more appropriate in learning what he calls the 'content'. This is a particular example of the general thesis that there need be no conflict between these different approaches to learning. The possible methods will depend largely on the details of what has to be learned (see Peters, 1969).

3 VIRTUES AND HABITS

Kohlberg maintains not only that character-traits such as honesty are comparatively unimportant in morals, but also that processes of habit formation, by means of which they are assumed to be established, are of secondary significance. The considerations which led him to this somewhat surprising view are as follows.

1. The Hartshorne–May investigation cast doubt upon the existence of stable character-traits. In the case of honesty, low predictability was shown of cheating in one situation from cheating in another. The tendency of children to cheat depended on the risk of detection and the effort required to cheat. Non-cheaters thus appeared to be more cautious rather than more honest. Peer-group approval and example also seemed to be an important determinant (Kohlberg, 1964, pp. 386–7).

2. Kohlberg claims that his own studies show that the decision not to cheat has something to do with the awareness of universal moral principles, not with principles concerned with the badness of cheating *per se*. Other good predictors of resistance to cheating are factors to do with ego strength. He concludes that the crucial determinants of moral development are cognitive. There are different conceptual levels in morality, and stability of character depends upon the level attained by the individual.

(a) *Traits and Principles*
Before discussing the role of habit in morality, something must

first be said about the dichotomy which Kohlberg makes between traits and principles. In his account of moral development a principled morality is contrasted with a morality of character-traits. This is a strange contrast. Surely, being just or fair are paradigm cases of character-traits. They are as much character-traits as being honest, which is the virtue with which justice is often contrasted in Kohlberg's work. Yet fairness and justice are also paradigm cases of moral principles. To call something a 'trait' of character is simply to suggest that someone has made a rule – for example, of honesty or of justice – his own. Whether a rule, which can also be regarded as a trait of character if it is internalised, is a principle depends on the function which the rule or consideration, which is personalised in the trait, performs. To call justice or concern for others principles is to suggest that backing or justification is provided by them for some more specific rule or course of action. We might, for instance, appeal to considerations of justice to back up a decision to give women the vote; gambling might be condemned because of the suffering which it brought on the relatives of gamblers. In these cases, justice and concern for others would be functioning as principles. Honesty, too, often functions as a principle in that it can be appealed to in condemning fraud and many other forms of deceit. The contrast, therefore, between traits of character and principles rests on no clear view of how the term 'principle' functions.

There is, however, an important contrast which Kohlberg does not make between traits, such as honesty and justice, and motives such as concern for others. As we shall see, there are important differences between virtues which are motives and those which are character traits. But one obvious difference needs to be noted at this point: that concern for others develops much earlier in a child's life and does not require the same level of conceptual development to be operative as does justice or even honesty. *Prima facie*, too, there are grounds for thinking that it can be learnt or encouraged by the example of others. Of course, concern for others can be exhibited at different levels which vary according to a person's imagination and sophistication about what constitutes harm or welfare. But it certainly can get a foothold in a person's moral life earlier than justice, because it is not necessarily connected with rules and social arrangements, as is justice. This was one of the reasons which led Hume to distinguish the artificial from the natural virtues. It may, of course, take time for children to grasp that reasons for rules can fall under it *as a principle*. Kohlberg's stage theory may apply to it in so far as it comes to function as a principle – that is, as providing considerations that give backing to rules. But a different account must be given of how children become sensitised to such considerations than is given of how they come to be concerned about justice.

In talking about a principled morality we must not only distinguish motives from character-traits such as justice and honesty. We must also note the peculiarities of a certain class of character-traits that are both content-free and which do not, like motives, introduce teleological considerations. These are traits such as consistency, persistence, courage, determination, integrity and the like. They are of a higher order and relate to the ways in which rules are followed or purposes pursued; they prescribe no particular rules or purposes, as do honesty and ambition. In ordinary language this group of character-traits is intimately connected with what we call 'the will'. Kohlberg suggests that 'ego-strength' variables correlate with the development of a principled morality. But this must necessarily be the case, for part of our understanding of a 'principled morality' is that people should stick to their principles in the face of temptation, ridicule and the like. But a different account must surely be given of their development than of that of a virtue like justice, for though it may be a necessary condition of a stable, principled morality that people should both be able to understand what justice is and assent to it, and that it should come to function as a principle for them in the sense of providing justifying reasons for a whole range of behaviour, it is nevertheless not sufficient. There are many who can do all this but who still lack the courage, determination, integrity and persistence to carry out what they see as just.

It looks, therefore, as if there is little validity in Kohlberg's distinction between principles and character-traits. But a more positive finding of this brief examination is that there are distinct classes of virtues, the differences between which may prove to be important in considering the relationships between virtue and habit. To summarise, there are (a) highly specific virtues, such as punctuality, tidiness and perhaps honesty, which are connected with specific types of acts, and which lack any built-in reason for acting in the manner prescribed – that is, are not motives, unlike (b) virtues, such as compassion, which are also motives for action. There are, then, (c) more artificial virtues, such as justice and tolerance, which involve more general considerations to do with rights and institutions. Finally, there are (d) virtues of a higher order, such as courage, integrity, perseverance, and the like, which have to be exercised in the face of counter-inclinations.

When, therefore, Kohlberg criticises a character-trait type of morality on account of the specificity of character-traits, it looks as if his criticism is based on the peculiar features of the character-trait of honesty, on which most research has been done. Dishonesty has to be understood in terms of fairly specific situations such as cheating, lying and fraud. This is a feature of all type (a) virtues. Other virtues and vices, however, such as benevolence, cruelty and integrity, are not tied down in this way to specific types of action, although about all such virtues the more sophisticated point could be made that what is to count as cases of them will vary from culture to culture. Kohlberg's criticism, therefore, depends on the peculiarities of a particular class of character-traits.

In general, however, this criticism follows analytically from the meaning attached to a principled morality; for principles pick out very general considerations, such as unfairness or harm to people, which can be appealed to in support of a number of rules. As many type (a) character-traits, such as thrift, punctuality, chastity and the like, represent internalised social rules whose justification depends upon appeal to more general considerations picked out by principles, their specificity, when compared with principles, is not surprising, for it is implicit in what we mean by a principle. But here again this depends very much on the examples taken. Punctuality and thrift manifestly require some further justification in terms of principles. Fairness and unselfishness, on the other hand, are also character-traits, but there is nothing particularly specific about them. Indeed, they are internalisations of considerations which would normally be appealed to as principles. Consistency, integrity, determination and the like are, as we have seen, character-traits as well, but of a higher order and in no way tied down to specific acts.

It is important to realise too, that although principles pick out abstract considerations that can be appealed to in contexts of justification and moral uncertainty, for the most part they enter into our lives in a much more concrete, specific way. For most of us, for instance, the principle that we should consider people's interests is to be understood by reference to specific roles such as that of a father, teacher, citizen, etc., with the specific duties that are constitutive of them, and in following the more general rules that are internalised in the form of punctuality, tidiness, thriftiness and the like. This was a point well made by Mill in his stress on the role of 'secondary principles' in morality.

(b) *The Role of Habit*
Kohlberg's contention that specific character-traits, such as honesty,

which function as habits, are of little significance in the moral life, is paralleled by his claim that learning theorists have produced no evidence of the influence of early forms of habit training on adult behaviour (Kohlberg, 1966). Most of the evidence is negative – the effect of exposure to Boy Scouts, Sunday School, etc., and of the effect of earliness and amount of parental training on habits such as obedience, neatness, etc. (Kohlberg, 1964, p. 388). This type of learning seems to be short-term, situation-specific and reversible.

This lack of importance assigned to habit goes against a whole tradition of thought about moral development stemming from Aristotle. He too assigned a central place to cognitive factors in moral development in so far as he characterised this in terms of the gradual emergence of practical reason. But he conceded a major role to habits in morals and in moral education. He maintained (Aristotle, Bk 11, Ch. 1) that the capacity given to us by nature to receive virtue is brought to maturity by habit. We acquire virtue by practice. Just as we become builders by building houses, so 'we become just by doing just acts, temperate by doing temperate acts, brave by doing brave acts' (Aristotle, Bk 11, Ch. 1). It is therefore of great importance to see that children are trained in one set of habits rather than another. In their early years they cannot, of course, act bravely or justly in a full sense for they lack the appropriate knowledge and dispositions. But through instruction, praise and blame, reward and punishment by men who are already courageous and just, they can acquire action patterns which gradually become informed by a growing understanding of what they are doing and why.

How then is habit related to virtue in the life of a developed person, and how can a morality, which is firmly rooted in habit, provide the appropriate basis for a more rational reflective type of morality? An examination of the concept of 'habit' may indicate answers to these questions which are also compatible with Kohlberg's contentions about habit formation; for it may well be the case that his contentions depend upon a limited conception of 'habit' and on the peculiarities of the facets of morality on which he has concentrated his attention.

In order to raise questions about the role of habit in morality, it is necessary to distinguish three applications of the concept of 'habit'. (See also Peters, 1963; Kazepides, 1969.) We can speak, first, in a descriptive way about a person's habits or what he does habitually. Secondly, we can use explanatory phrases such as 'out of habit', 'from force of habit', and 'a matter of sheer habit'. Thirdly, we can talk of certain things being learnt by a process of 'habituation'. Let us consider each of these applications of the concept of 'habit' in relation to the types of virtue already distinguished in section 3(a).

Habits When we use 'habit' as a descriptive term, we are making certain suggestions about behaviour. We are claiming, first, that it is something that the individual has done before and is likely to do again. It implies repetition arising from a settled disposition. Secondly, we suggest that it is the sort of thing that the individual *can* carry out more or less automatically. He does not have to reflect about it before he does it, to plan it in any way, or to decide to do it. But he may. If one of a man's habits is to get up early, it does not follow that he will not reflect about it on a particular occasion. It only suggests that he will not *have* to reflect on what he is doing on a particular occasion, that he *can* do this more or less automatically. Needless to say, also, there are many manifestations of automatic behaviour that are not usually habits – for example, automatic writing.

What forms of behaviour can be termed 'habits'? Etymologically, the word suggests forms of behaviour that one has in the way in which one has clothes. Habits, like clothes, express how a man holds himself. They thus can refer to his demeanour as well as to his clothes. Nowadays, we tend to confine the word to a person's settled dispositions which manifest themselves in behaviour which, like clothes, he can put on or take off at will. We do not, therefore, call dreaming a habit, nor do we speak in this way of stomach-aches and facial tics. We thus can say that a man is in the habit of going for a walk before breakfast, that talking philosophy in the pub is one of his habits, or that he is habitually punctual and polite.

There are some forms of behaviour which may be exercises of dispositions which we do not call 'habits'. For instance, we do not talk about sympathetic or angry behaviour as 'habits'. This is because these forms of behaviour are too deeply connected with our nature; they are not the sorts of behaviour that we can put on and take off at will, like clothes. Also they are not the sorts of behaviour which, even if repeated, we tend to perform automatically. If we did, they would cease to qualify as being sympathetic or angry in a full-blooded sense.

It might be thought that there is an incompatibility between habits and intelligence or reasoning. But if there is such a clash, it is not with this application of the concept of 'habit'. Ryle (1948, pp. 42-3), for instance, sees such an incompatibility. But that is because he does not distinguish between the three applications of the concept of 'habit'.

He slides between talking descriptively of habits, which he regards as single-track dispositions, and the use of explanatory phrases such as 'out of habit'. He also seems to think that all habits are developed by a particular form of habituation, namely drill, and incorporates this mistaken empirical assumption into his concept of 'habit'. In actual fact, not all habits are single-track dispositions. Playing bridge or chess could be regarded as among a person's habits, and there is nothing single-track or unintelligent about activities of this sort. Indeed, there are writers who go to the opposite extreme. Oakeshott, for instance, regards plasticity as one of the main features of habits. To use his own words: 'Like prices in a free market, habits of moral behaviour show no revolutionary changes because they are never at rest' (Oakeshott, 1962, p. 65). Habitual forms of behaviour can involve reasoning as well as intelligence in the sense of adaptability. Indeed, we can talk about a habit of reflecting upon conduct.

Is there any reason, then, why virtues should not be described as habits, and are they of much importance in morality? Surely the importance of established habits in the moral life is manifest. Life would be very exhausting if, in moral situations, we always had to reflect, deliberate and make decisions. It would also be very difficult to conduct our social lives if we could not count on a fair stock of habits such as punctuality, politeness, honesty and the like, in other people. This applies particularly to those type (a) character-traits, such as punctuality and tidiness, which are internalised social rules.

Habits, however, are not sufficient for the conduct of a person's moral life for at least three reasons. The first reason is that the different classes of virtues distinguished in section 3(a) differ in their relation to habit, and it is important to understand what underlies Kohlberg's claim that only some situation-specific types of virtue, which form part of the 'content' of morality, can be habits. Type (a) virtues, such as punctuality, tidiness and perhaps honesty, seem to be the most obvious class of virtues which can be called habits, because they are connected with specific types of acts; so there seems to be no difficulty about the condition of automaticity being sometimes fulfilled. They also lack any built-in reason for acting in the manner prescribed. They are to be contrasted with type (b) virtues, such as compassion, which are also motives for action. It seems essential to the exercise of such virtues that feelings should be aroused, that one's mind should be actively employed on bringing about specific states of affairs. The concept of 'habit' therefore cannot get a grip on virtues such as these. Nor can it get a grip on type (c), more artificial virtues, such as justice and tolerance, for a rather different reason. Being just, tolerant, or prudent involves much in the way of thought. Considerations have to be weighed and assessed. The suggestion, therefore, that acting justly might be one of a man's habits sounds strange. Finally, type (d), higher-order virtues, such as courage, integrity, perseverance and the like, would also be incongruously described as habits, because such virtues have to be exercised in the face of counter-inclinations. It is, of course, part of our understanding of what can be considered a virtue that there should be counter-inclinations which might be operative. Otherwise there would be no point in the virtue in general. But it is only essential to some virtues, namely, those that involve some kind of self-control, that counter inclinations must be present when they are exercised. Now in so far as this condition is realised, as it is in the case of virtues such as courage, it seems inappropriate to think of them as habits, for they require active attention. This would not be true, however, of all higher-order virtues – for example, consistency, which might be regarded as a habit.

The second reason for the insufficiency of habit in the moral life is that those virtues which we can call habits have an incompleteness about them because the reason for behaving in the ways which they mark out is not internal to them, which is why we do not call virtues such as thrift, punctuality and politeness motives. It is not surprising therefore, that the Hartshorne–May enquiry found that children saw being honest as a way of escaping punishment or gaining approval. These may not be particularly good reasons for acting honestly, but some reason is required; people do not act *out of* honesty, as they act out of jealousy or compassion. Honesty, in other words, is a trait of character, not a motive. Ideally, acting honestly should be connected with considerations which provide a rationale for being honest, rather than considerations which are manifestly extrinsic to this form of behaviour, such as the avoidance of punishment or the obtaining of approval. But such a rationale is beyond the understanding of young children. So it is not surprising that, in so far as they are honest, they are honest for some extrinsic reason, as Aristotle saw in his account of how virtues are acquired under instruction.

This introduces a third point about the insufficiency of habits – when people are in non-routine situations, habits, by definition, can no longer carry them through. The question then arises, with virtues such as honesty and punctuality, as to what considerations become operative. If, as in the case of the children in the Hartshorne–May enquiry, or that of the Spartans when they went abroad, the sanctions of punishment and social approval are withdrawn, they may not continue to be honest. In their case the extrinsic considerations which supported their honesty were not such that honesty seemed sensible to them when being dishonest had no manifest disadvantages and some short-term advantage. Suppose, however, that, as Aristotle put it, 'they understand the reason why of things', and connect being honest with some more general principle about human relationships – for example, respect for persons, concern for finding out what is true. They might then link particular manifestations of honesty, such as not cheating, or not lying, with further considerations falling under these principles. This would be what Kohlberg calls having a 'principled morality' which, he claims, is the only stable sort. He usually links this with the acceptance of the principle of justice, but this is only a particular case of such a morality. What is important is that considerations deriving from such principles are reasons which always exist for various ways of being honest. Possible censure or punishment, on the other hand, do not always exist and they depend on the attitude of people generally to breaches of rules such as that of honesty. They provide reinforcements for rules rather than a rationale. If people have no rationale for rules, and only keep to them in conditions where there is positive or negative reinforcement for them, then they are ill-equipped to deal with situations of a non-routine sort where the usual reinforcements are absent. This points to the necessity for the development of reason in morals to provide a rationale for habit. Reason is a supplement to habit but not a substitute for it.

Out of Habit   It was noted that there seems to be no incompatibility between 'habit', when used as a descriptive term, and intelligence and reasoning. But there is a clash when explanatory terms such as 'out of habit' are used of behaviour; for this phrase and others, such as 'from force of habit', do suggest routine types of situations to which the concept of 'intelligence' is not applicable. The condition of automaticity, of a stereo-typed form of behaviour, seems more strongly implied. They also rule out the possibility that the individual who has done something has deliberated before he did it, has reflected or gone through any process of self-criticism or justification, or has seen what he does as a means to a further end. Of course he might, in the past, have formed this particular habit by some series of decisions involving deliberation, planning, justification and other such exercises of reason. But if we say that a man does something, for instance, calls someone 'sir' out of habit, we are denying that in this case any of the processes typically associated with reason have taken place. He might be able to give *a* reason for this if asked afterwards, but on this particular occasion he did not act with the end in view which he might specify if so pressed; it was not *his* reason.

'Out of habit' also rules out explanations of behaviour which relate to features intrinsic to the behaviour so explained. In other words, it rules out the suggestion that the individual did what he did for enjoyment, because of the satisfaction which it brought him, or for fun. It also rules out any suggestion of its being done out of a sense of duty. It claims nothing more than that this is the sort of thing that the individual tends to do because he has done it often before. To put it more technically, the explanation is in terms of the old psychological law of exercise.

In the life of any man, however rational, it is important that a great many things should be done out of habit. His mind is then set free to pay attention to things that are novel and interesting, and for which he has no established routine. Any complex skill, for instance, presupposes a number of component movements that are performed out of habit, and conversation would flag at meal times if most of our eating manœuvres were not performed out of habit. But what about the sphere of morality? Has this application of the concept of 'habit' much relevance to this sphere?

Everything that was previously said about virtues which can be called habits would apply also *a fortiori* to the suggestion that they might be exercised out of habit. The only difference would be that more might be ruled out because the condition of automaticity seems to be more strongly suggested. To say that something is a habit is to say that it is the sort of behaviour that an individual *could* perform without giving his mind to it, but to say that he performed it out of habit is to suggest that he did not give his mind to it. Obviously, therefore, type (b) virtues, which are motives, type (c) virtues, which involve much in the way of thought, and type (d) virtues, which involve self-control, would be ruled out. But even some type (a) virtues might seldom be exercised out of habit. Honesty, for instance, is exercised by means of a specific range of acts such as telling the truth, not cheating and so on. But it would not often be exercised out of habit, because people are usually honest in the face of some sort of temptation, though they might be so disciplined that they become almost oblivious of this aspect of the situation. Honesty does not *have* to be exercised in the face of some counter-inclination as does a type (d) virtue such as courage. Thus, in a particular case, a man might be honest without being troubled much by counter-inclinations, and it might be said of him that he was honest out of habit. But this explanation of behaviour is appropriate, in the main, to the more conventional virtues such as politeness, punctuality and thrift.

Habituation Thus far I have considered only one problem raised both by Aristotle and by Kohlberg, namely, that of the relationship between virtue and habit in the moral life. We must now address ourselves to another problem, that of the development of a rational morality out of a basis provided by early habit formation. In other words, we must study the relationship between the development of virtues and various forms of habituation.

Kohlberg, like Plato, emphasises that the most important features of moral education are cognitive. The individual has to come to the grasp of principles and to connect particular rules like that of honesty with these instead of with extrinsic reinforcements such as praise and blame, reward and punishment. A grasp of principles, he maintains, cannot be directly taught; it can only develop with appropriate environmental stimulation, like the grasp of the causal principle or of the conservation of material things. This confirms Aristotle's point that children cannot, in the early stages of their lives, behave like the just man. This means two things: first, that they cannot grasp the principle of justice, which is very abstract and difficult to grasp; and secondly, that they cannot raise questions about the validity of rules, that they cannot see that principles, such as that of justice, might provide a justification for other rules. As Piaget (1932) showed, it takes quite a time in the development of children before the notion of the validity of rules makes any sense to them, before they realise that they might be otherwise, and those rules they accept should depend upon the rationale which can be provided. Thus, in their early years, they cannot accept rules in a rational way or be taught rules by processes, such as explanation and persuasion, which depend upon the ability to grasp a rationale.

What, then, is to be said about early moral education? Must children first of all become habituated to following certain rules, as Aristotle suggested, and can we conceive of a form of behaviour which is learned in this way, developing into the rational form of behaviour of Aristotle's just man or into Kohlberg's principled type of morality? We must first ask what is meant by 'habituation'. We use the term to describe a wide class of learning processes in which people learn by familiarising themselves with, or getting used to, things, and by repetition. For instance, a boy might learn not to be afraid of dogs by a process of habituation, by being constantly in their presence and getting used to their ways. This type of learning might be contrasted with being instructed or with learning by insight. Drill is another obvious example of habituation.

Ryle, as has already been mentioned, not only thinks that habits are formed by the particular process of habituation known as drill, but incorporates this belief into the meaning of 'habit'. This raises the question whether habits must be formed by *some* process of habituation, even if it is not the particular process of drill. It does not look as if this is a conceptual truth. Indeed, the *Oxford English Dictionary* explicitly states that there is no etymological ground for supposing that a habit must even be an acquired tendency. One might be led to think this because part of our understanding of 'habit' is that a form of behaviour should be repeated. We might therefore conclude that it was learned by repetition. But this is not necessarily the case. After puberty, for instance, one of a boy's habits might be to look long and lingeringly at pretty girls. He did not have to learn to do this. He just found himself doing it. The explanation would be in terms of the maturation of the sex organs and consequent sensitisation to girls, rather than in terms of any process of habituation, let alone drill.

Most habits, however, as a matter of empirical fact, are learned by some process of habituation. Not all of these are characterised by the sort of mindlessness that we associate with drill. If this was the case, the emergence of any rational type of morality out of processes of habituation would be a mystery. For instance, after reflection on the unsatisfactoriness of his daily pattern of life, a man can make a resolution to get up early; he can decide to make this one of his habits. In the early stages, when the alarm sounds, he may have to exhort himself, to rehearse his reasons for getting up early, and so on. When he has formed the habit, none of this deliberation and decision is necessary; but this is one way of forming a habit. Similarly, we can form habits intelligently in the context of an activity which has some overall end, such as a game of tennis. We may have to drill ourselves in particular movements, but we can learn also to make the movements in the context of a more widely conceived objective – for example, putting the ball where the opponent is not. Indeed, practice in situations where movements have to be varied in the light of changes in the situation is regarded by many as one of the best ways of forming habits, for this prevents too stereotyped a pattern of movements developing. Important, also, in the development of adaptable habits are the higher-order scruples connected with reason, such as having regard to whether what is done is correct, taking care, checking and thinking of objections. These scruples are learned mainly by taking part in situations where actions and performances are criticised. Gradually, through a process of role-playing, the learner becomes a constant critic of his own performances.

These ways of forming habits, in which reason and intelligence are involved, can be contrasted with other processes of habituation where a habit is 'picked up' in ways which are explicable only in terms of laws of association, such as contiguity, recency and frequency. In these cases, the learner may not be trying to master anything; there may even be a suggestion of automaticity. Something is done, for instance, which is associated with something pleasant, and it is repeated as in operant conditioning. Or some constant conjunction leads the individual to expect something without any connection being consciously noted – for example, the part played by serial probability in learning to spell. Alternatively, some mannerism, or form of behaviour, is picked up by some process of imitation without any conscious modelling or copying. These principles may also be at work in cases where habits are deliberately formed, or where a person's mind is on what is being learnt. This is not being denied. For instance, in learning to spell, one can attempt to learn in a rational way by formulating rules. This can help learning; but at the same time one may also learn through 'picking up' combinations of letters which frequently occur together. The point is that there are some processes of habituation where people fall into habits in ways which are explicable purely in terms of associative principles. But not all cases of habituation are like this.

Learning the Content of Morality: Type (a) *Virtues*   What then is to be said about the role of 'habituation' in the moral sphere? Surely, it cannot refer to a process in which learning is explicable purely in terms of the principles of association. For, as in all cases of learning, one cannot apply some general theory of learning without paying careful attention to what it is that has to be learnt. And this is very complicated in the moral case, even if we take some type (a) virtue, as honesty, which is to form part of the content of morality. Learning to be honest is not like learning to swim. It could not conceivably be picked up just by practice or by imitation; for a child has to understand what honesty is in order to behave in this way, and this presupposes all sorts of other concepts such as truth and falsehood, belief and disbelief, and so on. Such understanding cannot grow just by repetition and familiarity, though they may aid it. Similarly, extrinsic reinforcements, working by principles of association, may strengthen a tendency to behave in accordance with a rule, but the child has to understand what particular feature of his behaviour is being singled out for attention. Parents often punish children for stealing, without appreciating that the child has not yet the grasp of concepts such as property, ownership, lending, giving and the like which enable him to understand that it is stealing for which he is being punished. Such extrinsic reinforcers may help to mark out the relevant features of behaviour by, as it were, underlining some aspect of it. But it is impossible to conceive how they could be sufficient to bring about understanding. Neither could understanding develop just through untutored 'learning from experience'; for 'honesty' can only be exercised in relation to socially defined acts such as cheating and lying, and these could not be understood without initiation into a whole network of social practices. There must, therefore, be some kind of teaching of rules for moral education to get started at all. The content has to be exhibited, explained, or marked out in some way which is intrinsically rather than extrinsically related to it. This is a central feature of any process that can be called a process of teaching. Moral education is inconceivable without some process of teaching, whatever additional help is provided by various processes of habituation.

Although at an early stage there is no possibility of reason in the sense of justification being operative, there is ample scope for intelligence, for learning to apply a rule like that of honesty to a variety of situations which are relevantly similar. In other words, the rule can be taught in such a way that children gradually come to see the similarity between actions like that of lying and cheating. Parents can relate rules to their point even if children do not yet grasp the idea that their validity depends upon their point. And, surely, drawing attention to the consequences of their actions will help them to understand that actions have consequences. This at least will prepare the way for the stage when they grasp that the reasons for some rules of action depends upon consequences.

Sensitisation to Principles: Type (b) *and* (c) *Virtues* Kohlberg maintains that the assessment of actions in terms of their consequences is an important feature of a developmental stage in morality that cannot be taught by any kind of direct instruction. Children, like Socrates' slave, must come to see it, which is true enough; for this is not just a matter of information, like the height of St Paul's cathedral, which simply has to be remembered rather than understood. But he also claims that 'cognitive stimulation' can aid this process of coming to understand. And what else is that, apart from presenting some kind of content in different ways until eventually the appropriate connections are made? And, in the case of rules, this is surely done by teaching them intelligently, that is, by linking rules with other rules and with consequences which will eventually come to be seen as providing some point for them. Kohlberg also argues that some features of the situation in which rules are learned, for example, parental warmth, aid cognitive development because they provide a favourable climate for it. It may also be the case that some sorts of extrinsic aids, such as punishment, may encourage a rigidity or lack of intelligence in rule following that may become compulsive. These, however, are empirical questions which are largely still a matter for speculation. All I have been trying to do is to show how it is intelligible that acquiring habits in ways that are possible at an early stage should develop into a more rational way of following rules. I have been putting the same kind of case in the sphere of morals that I previously put when discussing the general relationship between forming habits and intelligence. It is not the case that habits have to be formed by a process like that of drill. They can be formed in the context of an activity which is more widely conceived. My argument is that learning habits in an intelligent way can be re-garded as providing an appropriate basis, in the moral case, for the later stage when rules are followed or rejected because of the justifi-cation that they are seen to have or lack.

The encouragement of intelligent rule-following, however, in rela-tion to what Kohlberg calls the content of morality, is not the only thing that can be done in the early stages to prepare the way for principled morality. For, although a child may not be able, early in life, to connect rules with those considerations which are picked out by principles, he can become sensitive to considerations which will later serve him as principles. Psychologists such as Piaget and Kohl-berg have failed to draw attention to this because of their pre-occupation with type (c) virtues such as the principle of justice, which picks out very abstract considerations that are very difficult for a small child to grasp. If, however, instead of justice, we consider the status of type (b) virtues such as concern for others, I think that we may look at moral education in a very different light. The plight of others is much easier to grasp, and concern for it develops much earlier in children. If such concern is encouraged early in children, it can come to function later on as one of the fundamental principles of morality, when the child reaches the stage of being able to grasp the connection between many rules and their effect on other people.

Can anything be done early by training to sensitise children in this respect? Habituation seems the wrong sort of term to use in this context; for the last thing we want is to habituate children to the sight of suffering. Possibly, however, by exposing them a bit to the sight of suffering in others, or rather by not shielding them from situations where they will be confronted by it in a first-hand way, their sensitivity to it may be sharpened. It might also be argued that children can be encouraged to form the habit of paying attention to people's suffering rather than just concentrating on their own projects. This habit of mind would not itself be a virtue. But it might predispose children to be influenced by compassion on specific occasions. Again, this is a matter of speculation, but this sphere of the cultivation of appropriate forms of sensitivity is certainly one of the most crucial areas in the development of a principled form of morality. It is pointless to encourage children to reflect about rules, and to link them with general considerations of harm and benefit, if these considerations do not act as powerful motives for the person who can perform such calculations.

The Development of Self-control: Type (d) *Virtues*   When Aristotle spoke of the importance of habituation in moral education, perhaps he had in mind the particular type (d) virtues which are intimately connected with self-control. Indeed, Von Wright (1963, Ch. VII) has explicitly suggested that *all* virtues are forms of self-control. Habituation may be very important in the development of this particular class of virtues in that it may be necessary for people to be tempted, or made fearful, by situations which appear to them in a certain light. The more familiar they become with such situations, and with the internal commotions which they occasion, the more likely people are to be led by a variety of considerations to control their immediate responses. In the case of small children, the proper reasons for self-control are not readily apparent, and they are unable to link the manner of behaviour with its proper justification. If, however, children are exposed to, for example, danger, and praised when they do not run away in terror, they may learn to control themselves for such extrinsic reasons. There is, of course, the danger that later on they will only display courage when the reinforcing conditions associated with the manner of behaviour are present. But it could be argued that familiarity with both the external features of dangerous situations and with the internal commotions, which such danger occasions in them, carries over into situations in later life when they appreciate the proper reasons for being courageous. Like Aristotle's child, who learns to be temperate by behaving temperately under instruction, they are preparing themselves, by going through the motions of self-control, for the stage when they will have a more inward understanding of the reasons for the pattern of behaviour that they are exhibiting. Habituation is important both in familiarising children with the features of such situations and in developing the relevant action patterns that will enable them to deal practically with the emotions that may be aroused instead of being overcome by them. Habituation may thus help to lay down a pattern of response that may be used in the service of more appropriate motives at a later stage.

Kohlberg nowhere deals with the development of this class of virtues which necessarily involve self-control. He might well claim, however, that even if people do learn to be courageous by some such process of habituation, there is no evidence of transfer. Like the Spartans they might display their courage only in very specific types of situations. Or people might become physically brave but moral cowards. To which it might be replied that, if moral courage is thought a desirable character-trait to develop, it is difficult to conceive how it could develop without some kind of practice. Maybe there is not necessarily much transfer from situations requiring physical courage to those requiring moral courage, but some account must be given of how moral courage is developed. In this sphere the individual has to learn to accommodate himself not to dangers that threaten him in a palpable physical way, but to social threats and pressures such as ridicule, disapproval, ostracism and so on. These sorts of reactions on the part of others can be evoked by a wide range of moral stances taken up by an individual. It is therefore possible for an individual to learn to cope with typical patterns of response on the part of others on the basis of a very limited number of issues on which he may make a stand. In other words, there is a built-in type of generality about this type of moral training. The English public school system of character training, derived from Thomas Arnold, is usually associated with team spirit and moral conformism. But equally strong in this tradition is the insistence that the individual should stick up for principles connected with 'fair play' in the face of group pressure. Does Kohlberg think that an individual can in fact adhere to his favoured principle of justice, when the screws are put on him, without some such training? And does he think that generations of British administrators, who, like the Romans, were able to maintain the rule of law with a fair degree of impartiality in situations where they were comparatively isolated and subject to social pressures, bribes, flattery, etc., were quite unaffected by the type of character training to which they were subjected at school? This seems, on the face of it, a most implausible assumption, but, of course, it would be an extremely difficult one to test.

Morality and the Development of Motivation   Sticking to a principle such as justice, however, should not be represented in too negative a light, as it might be by those who are overinfluenced by the Puritan tradition. There is also strong positive aspect to it which is of great importance in considering the phenomenon of 'will'. This links with another central aspect of morality, to which Kohlberg pays too little attention, namely, the intimate connection between knowing the difference between right and wrong, and caring. It is not a logical contradiction to say that someone knows that it is wrong to cheat but has no disposition not to cheat, but it could not be the general case; for the general function of words like 'right' and 'wrong', 'good' and 'bad' is to move people to act. If there is no such disposition to act in a particular case, we would say that the person is using the term in an external sort of way, or that he is not sincere, or something similar to that. There is neither need nor time to defend such a generally accepted point about moral knowledge, though there has been no general acceptance, ever since the time that Socrates first put it forward, about the precise relationship between moral knowledge and action (see Ryle, 1958).

Now, as Hume pointed out, justice is an artificial virtue which only gets off the ground when reason gets to work in social life. Hume equated 'reason' with reasoning of the sort that goes on either in logic and mathematics or in science, and was led to think, therefore, that reason of itself provides no considerations that move people to act. On a broader view of 'reason', however, it becomes readily apparent that there are a cluster of 'passions' closely connected with it without which its operation would be unintelligible. I am referring not just to the passion for truth, but also to other passions which are intimately connected with it such as the abhorrence of the arbitrary, the hatred of inconsistency and irrelevance, the love of clarity and order, and, in the case of non-formal reasoning, the determination to look at the facts. These passions both provide point to theoretical enquiries and transform the pursuit of practical purposes.

When Kohlberg talks of the principle of justice, it is not clear whether he means the formal principle that no distinctions should be made without relevant differences or more particularised versions of this in distributive or commutative justice. But any application of this principle must involve some kind of abhorrence of arbitrariness and of inconsistency if it is to be operative in any individual's life. Also, as Kohlberg maintains that it presupposes becoming aware of some 'universal structural dimensions in the social world', some focused attention to the facts of the social world is also involved. How do such rational passions develop? What helps to foster them? Kohlberg, like Piaget, postulates some kind of intrinsic motivation which leads children to assimilate and accommodate to what is novel and to develop their latent capacities. But there is a great difference between sporadic curiosity and the passions which cluster round the concern for truth. Does not the encouragement and example of adults and older children play any part in their development? Without them a child's understanding of justice would be very external. He might know what justice is, but might not care about it overmuch. To apply the principle seriously, the child has to develop not only an abhorrence of the arbitrary, but also a more positive concern for the considerations that determine relevance. How do children come to care? This seems to me to be the most important question in moral education; but no clear answer to it can be found in Kohlberg's writings.

4 IS KOHLBERG PRESCRIBING A MORALITY?

In discussing the adequacy of Kohlberg's account of the role of habit in moral development, distinctions were made between different classes of virtues. These seemed to be of some significance in assessing his account of processes of development. But they are of even more fundamental significance if we survey Kohlberg's conception of moral development from an overall ethical standpoint; taking these distinctions seriously might lead us to reflect that Kohlberg is really prescribing one type of morality among several possibilities. 'Morality' can be used as a classificatory term by means of which a form of interpersonal behaviour can be distinguished from custom, law, religious codes and so on. But in ethics and in the practical task of bringing up children, this does not take us very far; for it would involve us in the most feeble form of the naturalistic fallacy to argue that, because we term a form of behaviour 'moral', this behaviour is one which should be pursued or encouraged. Nothing about what ought to be or to be done follows from the empirical fact that we use a word in a certain way. It might well be, for instance, that a form of behaviour, in which justice plays such a prominent part, might accord very well with our usage of 'moral'. But that is neither here nor there if anyone is troubled by the general question, 'What are there reasons for doing?' or by more particular questions about how he is to bring up his children.

Even within this principled form of morality considered thus far, there are, in fact, different emphases open. For instance, one might think that the most important things to encourage in children were sympathy, compassion, concern for others and the like. One might not be particularly concerned about consistency or about the virtue of justice, which one might think of as being a rather niggardly one. Similarly, one might think that courage, integrity, autonomy, or other such excellences ought to be encouraged without being overly concerned about the substantial rules or purposes in relation to which these higher-order traits were exercised. Finally, one might not be too impressed with the interpersonal realm. One might go along with Gauguin and say that painting pictures was the thing, or advocate some other type of worthwhile activity. This form of activity, it might be said, is so valuable that considerations of an interpersonal sort would have to be set aside. All of these are possible moral positions in the general sense that reasons could be given for behaving in the ways suggested and for bringing up one's children accordingly. Of course, an attempt might be made to introduce some kind of unity into the moral life either by attempting to show that all such considerations were derived from one type of consideration, as did the Utilitarians, or by arbitrarily demarcating the sphere of the moral, as did Kant. But *prima facie* it appears to be a difficult enterprise, and it is certainly not one upon which Kohlberg has embarked. His account of moral development might therefore be considered to be one-sided in that it has been erected on the features of a limited interpretation of morality.

A further point must be made, too, about any moral system in which justice is regarded as the fundamental principle: it cannot be applied without a view, deriving from considerations other than those of justice, about what is important. This point can be demonstrated only very briefly, but it is one of cardinal importance. When we talk about what is just or unjust, we are applying the formal principle of reason – that no distinctions should be made without relevant differences, either to questions of distribution, when we are concerned about the treatment which different people are to receive, or to commutative situations, when we are concerned not with comparisons but with questions of desert, as in punishment. In all such cases some criterion has to be produced by reference to which the treatment is to be based on *relevant* considerations. There must therefore be some further evaluative premise in order to determine relevance. Without such a premise, no decisions can be made about what is just on any substantive issue. In determining, for instance, what a just wage is, relevant differences must be determined by reference to what people need, to what they contribute to the community, to the risk involved, and so on. To propose any such criteria involves evaluation. This opens up obvious possibilities for alternative emphases in morality in addition to those already mentioned. But are these emphases to be put on the 'formal' or on the 'content' side of Kohlberg's account of moral development? When we begin to look at his system in this more detailed way, it must become apparent that it is either implicitly prescriptive or so formal that it is of only limited significance for those who are interested in moral education, or moral development, in a concrete way. His findings are of unquestionable importance, but there is a grave danger that they may become exalted into a general theory of moral development. Any such general theory presupposes a general ethical theory, and Kohlberg himself surely would be the first to admit that he has done little to develop the details of such a general ethical theory. Yet without such a theory the notion of 'moral development' is pretty insubstantial.

5 FREUD AND MORAL FAILURE

It would be impossible in a short space to do justice to Kohlberg's massive examination of theories deriving from Freud which explain moral development in terms of identification (Kohlberg, 1963). But one main point can be made which is in line with the general thesis of this article: Kohlberg assumes that Freudians must be in some way producing an alternative theory to his own Piagetian theory of moral development. No doubt many Freudians have thought that they were doing this, and some of Freud's speculations in this area might support such a view. But, as I have maintained elsewhere (see Peters, 1960), it is equally plausible to maintain that, in fact, Freud was attempting explanations of a rather different realm of phenomena.

Rieff (1959) makes much of what he calls Freud's ethic of honesty and of his uncompromising egoism. He suggests that Freud's 'education to reality' and his explicit advocacy of 'the primacy of the intelligence' amounted to a prudential type of morality in which self-honesty played a large part. This, as a matter of fact, is a disputable interpretation of Freud's own moral standpoint. He actually said of himself, 'I believe that in a sense of justice and consideration for others, in disliking making others suffer or taking advantage of them I can measure myself with the best people I know' (Jones, 1955, p. 464), which looks very much like the confession of a rational Utilitarian sort of code that one could find in Sidgwick – or indeed in Piaget. But what is not disputable is that Freud subscribed to some sort of rational morality, which his practice as a therapist also presupposed; for the aim of psycho-analysis was to strengthen the ego by making unconscious conflicts conscious and by helping people to stand on their own feet with full cognisance of the sources of their irrational promptings and precepts. But in his theory of moral development there is no explicit theory about the development of the ego, which, in Freud's rather pictorial terminology, represented a rational level of behaviour. Indeed, he was later criticised by Freudians such as Erikson, Hartmann and Rapaport for neglecting the development of the autonomous ego, the stages of which were mapped in Piaget's theory.

What, then, did Freud's theory of moral development explain? This is not at all a simple question, for Freud's theory underwent many transformations (see Flugel, 1945). One might say, for instance, that the early theory of the ego ideal was meant to explain simply how some kind of cultural *content* was passed on from parents to children by the rather mysterious process of identification. And even this limited interpretation would not be inconsistent with Kohlberg's theory in that Kohlberg is not much interested in content; from his point of view identification might be as good or as bad an explanation of the transmission of *content* as habit formation. For Kohlberg, it will be remembered, argues that it is the *form* of moral experience rather than its content which is of crucial developmental significance. But Freud was not basically concerned with a simple theory of content transmission in his theory of the ego ideal, let alone in his later speculations about the super-ego. On the one hand, he was trying to explain the fact that some children seem to develop more rigorous standards than those demanded by their parents; on the other hand, he tried to explain the fact that many people have a picture of themselves – what Adler later called a 'guiding fiction' – which is quite out of keeping with the traits which they in fact exhibit. In other words, Freud's theory of the super-ego was basically a theory of moral failure – of why people become obsessional, unrealistic and aggressively self-punitive in the moral sphere. It therefore can be seen as a supplement to Piaget's type of theory rather than as a substitute for it.

The same sort of point can be made about Freud's theory of character-traits. This does not begin to look like a theory of how traits such as honesty, which were studied in the Hartshorne – May enquiry, are developed. Nor is it a theory about the development of higher-order traits such as consistency, determination and courage, to which we are usually alluding when we speak of people *having* character. Rather, it is in the tradition of characterology, which goes right back to Theophrastus, in which a type of character is portrayed. Either there is a subordination of traits to a dominant one, as in the sketch of the penurious man; or a whole range of traits are shown as being exercised in an exaggerated or distorted manner, as in the case of a pedantic person. Jones (1955, p. 331) explicitly speaks of Freud's *Character and Anal Erotism* as a contribution to this sort of speculation, and he notes its literary style. Freud thought that he spotted a similarity between types of character and various forms of neuroses, and assigned a common cause to both in his theory of infantile sexuality. Here again we do not have a competing explanation of the sort of phenomena in which Kohlberg is interested, namely, the determinants of a rational, principled form of morality. Rather we have an attempt to explain types of character that fall a long way short of this in some systematic way.

To discuss the status of the evidence for Freud's type of explanation, even for this realm of deviant phenomena, would require another article – and it would not be the sort that a philosopher would be expected to write. But these phenomena exist, and they certainly cannot be explained in terms of either Kohlberg's or Piaget's type of theory. Therefore, in so far as Freud and his followers have been attempting explanations, however far-fetched, of phenomena of this sort, they are providing a much needed supplement to the work of the Piaget–Kohlberg school. It is not doing justice to them to represent them as providing merely a competing theory of moral development.

BIBLIOGRAPHY

Aristotle, *Nichomachean Ethics*. See Thompson, J. A. K. (Ed.) (Harmondsworth: Penguin, 1955).

Flugel, J. C., *Man, Morals and Society* (London: Duckworth, 1945).

Jones, E., *Sigmund Freud, Life and Works*. Vol. II (London: Hogarth Press, 1955).

Kazepides, A. C., 'What is the Paradox of Moral Education?', *Philosophy of Education 1969*. Proceedings of the twenty-fifth annual meeting of the Philosophy of Education Society (Denver, 1969).

Kohlberg, L., 'Moral Development and Identification', in Stevenson, H. (Ed.),

Child Psychology. 62nd Yearbook Nat. Soc. Stud. Educ. (Chicago: University of Chicago Press, 1963).

Kohlberg, L., 'Development of Moral Character and Ideology', in Hoffman, M. L. (Ed.), *Review of Child Development Research*.Vol. I (New York: Russell, Sage Foundation, 1964).

Kohlberg, L., 'Moral Education in the Schools', *School Review*, Vol. 74 (1966), pp. 1–30.

Kohlberg, L., 'Stage and Sequence: The Cognitive–Developmental Approach to Socialization', in Goslin, D. (Ed.), *Handbook of Socialization* (New York: Rand McNally, 1968).

Kohlberg, L. 'Early Education: A Cognitive Developmental View', *Child Development*, Vol. 39 (1968), pp. 1013–62.

Kohlberg, L., 'Education for Justice', in Sizer, N. F. and Sizer, T. R. (Eds), *Moral Education* (Cambridge, Mass.: Harvard University Press, 1970).

Kohlberg, L., 'Stages in the Development of Moral Thought and Action', unpublished manuscript.

Oakeshott, M. (Ed.), 'The Tower of Babel', in *Rationalism in Politics* (London: Methuen, 1962).

Peters, R. S., 'Freud's Theory of Moral Development in Relation to That of Piaget', *British Journal of Educational Psychology*, Vol. 30 (1960), pp. 250–8.

Peters, R. S., 'Reason and Habit: The Paradox of Moral Education', in Niblett, W. R. (Ed.), *Moral Education in a Changing Society* (London: Faber, 1963).

Peters, R. S. (Ed.), *Perspectives on Plowden* (London: Routledge, 1969).

Piaget, J., *The Moral Judgment of the Child* (London: Routledge, 1932).

Rieff, P., *Freud, the Mind of the Moralist* (New York: Viking Press, 1959).

Ryle, G., *The Concept of Mind* (London: Hutchinson, 1948).

Ryle, G., 'On Forgetting the Difference Between Right and Wrong', in Melden, A. I. (Ed.), *Essays in Moral Philosophy* (Seattle: University of Washington Press, 1958).

Von Wright, G. H., *The Varieties of Goodness* (London: Routledge, 1963).

Chapter 6

Freedom and the Development of the Free Man[1]

There is a presupposition implicit in the writings and practices of educators which is of interest in its own right and to educational theory generally. It is that some desirable state of mind or character-trait will be best developed by an institution whose workings reflect the principle, which is thought desirable when personalised as a character-trait. Thus Plato assumed that justice in the individual soul would flourish in society whose organisation satisfied the conditions required by this principle. The institution of punishment has been defended on similar grounds. It is claimed that it is a manifest exemplar of justice and that children who witness its operation will receive the imprint of justice on their minds. Alternatively it is assumed that if certain procedures characterise the working of an institution (e.g. rules decided by appeals to authority, by democratic discussion, etc.) corresponding attitudes of mind will be fostered amongst its members. A. S. Neill, for instance, assumes that his ideal of self-regulation or freedom of the individual will be best developed in an institution in which external regulation is at a minimum, and in which such regulation as there is does not stem from the authority of adults.

It is this type of assumption which, in my view, lies behind the intuitive plausibility of so much educational argument. A. S. Neill is actually very guarded in his claims for the long-term effects of Summerhill on its inmates. And what he does claim is based purely on selective impressions. He had conducted no surveys to find out how many of his previous pupils have succumbed to the 'fear of freedom', and ended up as members of the Communist Party, the Catholic Church or as conformists. Nevertheless, he persists with his type of school and, I suspect, would be absolutely unconvinced by negative evidence of this mundane sort. He would offer some special explanation of cases in which children of servile dispositions issue forth from an institution in which freedom, as a social principle, is 'writ large'.

There are, as far as I know, no empirical studies which can be produced to test this assumption. Yet the interesting point is that considerations can be produced to support or to cast doubt on its plausibility. By examining what is meant by 'freedom' in a social context, like that of a school, and what is meant by a 'free man', some suggestions can be made about the connection between the two. To connect them some assumptions would also have to be made about human learning. But I must not, by developing this point any further at this stage, anticipate one of the main points which I want to discuss in this paper. For it has a three-fold intention behind it. I propose to take 'freedom' as an example of the general assumption about the fit between institutions and states of mind. To develop my general thesis I will first examine the concept or concepts of 'freedom' in education and distinguish the various things that might be meant. Secondly I will explore what is involved in learning to be free, including the status of the presupposition about the influence of institutions on learning in this sphere. This will lead, finally, to a few general reflections about human learning arising from this particular case of it.

1 THE ANALYSIS OF 'FREEDOM'

In approaching these questions I shall attempt no new analysis of 'freedom'. In the main I shall rely on the distinctions already worked out by Stanley Benn[2] and William Weinstein: (a) freedom as a social principle, (b) man as a chooser, (c) autonomy, which are particularly helpful in an educational context. My use of their analysis, however, will be strictly tailored to its relevance for discussing how individuals learn to be free.

(a) *Freedom as a Social Principle*
If we say that a man is not free to do something we are suggesting that there is something or somebody that is stopping him. We assume that there is something that he might want or choose to do and we suggest that there is some closing up of the options available to him.

The most obvious way of closing up a person's options is to restrict his bodily movements by tying him up or imprisoning him. But more usual ways are the making of laws and regulations, giving him commands, and subjecting him to a variety of social and personal pressures.

It is a common-place of political theory that the state of natural freedom is an illusion. If there are no levelling constraints like those of law and custom, men do not in fact live unconstrained lives. Those who are physically or psychologically weak are constrained by those who are strong. In spheres, therefore, in which people care what others do and in which it is possible for them to interfere with them, freedom in fact prevails only if there is a general system of regulation which safeguards these spheres against interference from others. This is an empirical generalisation derivative from certain facts about human nature and the conditions under which men live. It is not, as many enemies of freedom have argued, a conceptual truth about the meaning of 'freedom'. For 'freedom' manifestly does not mean the acceptance of constraints. It is just a general empirical fact that the acceptance of some forms of constraint by all is necessary for the avoidance of more grievous forms of constraint by some others. This so-called 'paradox of freedom' is extremely relevant to a school situation; for the constraints of the bully or the peer-group take over if the more explicit levelling constraints issuing from the staff or from the community as a whole, are withdrawn.[3] There are also more subtle forms of social pressure – e.g. those issuing from a charismatic teacher who may believe fervently in freedom – which may be more damaging to freedom in a more fundamental sense, than the straightforward exercise of authority. What, then, is this sense?

(b)   *Man as a Chooser*

Presupposed by this analysis of 'freedom' as a social principle is the notion of man as a chooser who can have his options closed up in various ways by the acts of other men. We speak of various spheres of authority as being spheres where individuals are not free to do as they please. Yet there is also an important connection between 'authority' and 'consent' or 'choice' as many writers in political theory have pointed out. We often, though not always, obey a command because we accord its author a right to tell us what to do. In the case of a voluntary club or association we do actually commit ourselves to its constitution and rules when we join it and we can leave it if we so choose. And in other spheres of authority, even if we have not explicitly committed ourselves in this way, it is open to us to reject the system as binding on us. Similarly if a person is playing football his freedom of action is limited by the rules and by the referee's decisions. But he can choose not to play football. There are difficulties, of course, about obedience to a state if there is nowhere to live that is not under the jurisdiction of some state. There are difficulties about leaving a place of employment if the alternative is the dole. But even in these dire extremities a person still remains a *chooser* even if the alternatives open to him are such that we might say that he has no choice or Hobson's choice.

In a school situation there are plenty of cases in which we would say that a student is not free to do certain things but that he still remains a chooser. For instance, he may not be free to run in the corridors, but he may, in fact, do so, knowing full well the penalty if he is caught. Indeed he may defy the whole system of rules and end up by being expelled. These situations of explicit subordination, or of refusal to be subordinated, need to be distinguished from those in which the notion of choice seems out of place. Suppose that a girl has an obsessive passion for a master. To do anything which he forbad, or of which he disapproved, would never enter her head. Indeed she might constantly look for things to do of which he approved and, if he told her to fast for a week or to steal, she would fall in with his wishes. In respect of her dealings with him she cannot really be described as a chooser; for alternatives that are presented to her are not really alternatives if they involve in any way going against his wishes. Like a person under post-hypnotic suggestion she may conjure up other alternatives and invent other reasons for doing what she is bent on doing anyway; but this is a mere shadow-play. She is really programmed to do what he wants. This kind of situation can exist in a school which has a normal authority structure; or it may exist in a progressive school that prides itself on the absence of such a structure. The lack of freedom involved is perhaps more dire than that of a situation structured by explicit regulation; for the girl is unfree in a more fundamental sense than are those who keep or break rules in a more straightforward way.

This type of case is a mild and usually short-term example of a range of cases about which we might say that an individual is no longer a chooser. They differ from the first application of 'freedom' to social situations in which what Benn calls the *objective* conditions of choice are interfered with or loaded in various ways – e.g. by threats, imposition of sanctions, etc. In this second type of case, in which we sometimes speak of 'unfreedom', men cease to be choosers, because there are various defects or interferences with the *subjective* conditions which are necessary for choice.

The forms of impairment to subjective conditions can roughly be indicated by setting out what we normally assume when people are in what I have elsewhere called a situation of practical reason, when they ask themselves the question 'Why do this rather than that?'[4]

(i) We assume that there is more than one type of end which can function for them as a goal. They do not, as it were, veer towards 'this' rather than 'that' like a moth towards a light. A man who had been starved for a week would probably not satisfy this condition. He would be 'driven' towards a goal. Drug addicts and alcoholics do not satisfy this condition in relation to a whole range of their deliberations.

(ii) We assume that people are capable of weighing the pros and cons of the alternatives before them without being paralysed by indecision or going out of the field in some other way. Some hysterics would not satisfy this condition.

(iii) We assume that the weight which people attach to different alternatives can be influenced by information which is relevant to the validity of their beliefs. Paranoiacs, or people suffering from other sorts of delusions or obsessions, would not satisfy this condition. For they hold on to beliefs in the face of relevant evidence, because their beliefs cannot deviate from the lines dictated by some irrational wish or aversion.

(iv) We assume that changes in people's beliefs about 'this' or 'that' can modify their decisions. A psychopath, for whom the future has a kind of unreality and who is unmoved by the unpleasantness which he sees to be the probable consequences of his actions, and which he wishes to avoid, would not qualify in this respect.

(v) We assume that people's decisions can be translated into appropriate actions. A compulsive would fail to satisfy this condition.

(c) *Autonomy*

Our normal expectation of a person is that he is a chooser – that he can be deterred by thoughts of the consequences of his actions, that he is not paranoid or compulsive and so on. But such a person might be a time-serving, congenial conformist, or an easy-going, weak-willed opportunist. Being a chooser is a standard expected of anyone – which is related to norms of rationality or mental health;[5] it is not an ideal of conduct or of education. Certainly progressive educators, such as A. S. Neill, who equates freedom with self-regulation, have been concerned with more than this limited objective. What, then, has to be added for a chooser to develop into an ideal type of character in which being free features? To ask this is to ask for the criteria for calling a person 'autonomous'.

Authenticity Etymologically 'autonomy' suggests that a person accepts or makes rules for himself. This is clear in what it denies but not altogether clear in what it asserts. It denies that the individual's code of conduct is simply one that he has picked up from others or adopted in any second-hand way. The rules which he lives by are not just those that are laid down by custom or authority. Hence the stress on authenticity going right back to Socrates' 'care of the soul'. This asserts positively that there must be some feature of a course of conduct, which the individual regards as important, which constitutes a non-artificial reason for pursuing it as distinct from extrinsic reasons provided by praise and blame, reward and punishment, and so on, which are artificially created by the demands of others. But beyond this point it is a matter of controversy as to what is asserted by the stress on autonomy. Presumably it would be consistent with a doctrine sometimes put into the mouth of D. H. Lawrence's characters that a course of conduct should be pursued that is congenial to the 'dark god' within, namely sex, which determines the lines of individual self-assertion. For this is represented as what the individual really wants as distinct from what conformity dictates. Or it would be consistent with some existentialist doctrine of 'criterionless choice', in so far as this can be rendered intelligible.

Rational Reflection More usually, however, autonomy is positively associated with assessment and criticism, as in Stanley Benn's account in his paper on 'Conditions of Autonomy'. The individual is conceived of as being aware of rules as alterable conventions which structure his social life. He subjects them to reflection and criticism in the light of principles and gradually emerges with his own code of conduct. This is the Kantian conception of autonomy in which the 'subjective maxims' of the individual are subjected to critical examination in the light of principles such as those of impartiality and respect for persons. This does not mean that he must always reflect before he acts and ponder on the validity of a rule which he is applying; for such a man would be a moral imbecile without settled principles. It only means that he has thought about rules in this way and has a disposition to do so if he finds himself in a situation where changed circumstances intimate some adaptation of his code.

Strength of Will   It is possible for a person to have a code of conduct which he has worked out for himself but to be too weak-willed to stick to it. Usually, however, when people speak of a person being autonomous they mean that he not only has thought out his own code but that he is also capable of sticking to it in the face of counter-inclinations. Autonomy, in other words, also suggests executive virtues such as courage, integrity and determination. It is revealed not simply in the refusal to adopt second-hand beliefs or rules, but also in holding steadfast in *conduct* against counter-inclinations which also incline an individual to be heteronomous in his point of view. For the counter-inclinations, which are relevant to weakness of will, are often those springing from types of motivation that make 'authenticity' in belief difficult. The strong-willed man, like the independently minded man, sticks to his principles in the face of ridicule, ostracism, punishment and bribes. There is thus a close connection between autonomy and strength of will but the connection is probably a contingent one to be explained in terms of the group of counter-inclinations that are necessary to give application both to the notion of authenticity and to that of strength of will.

There is thus a gradation of conditions implicit in the idea of autonomy. The first basic condition is that of authenticity, of adopting a code or way of life that is one's own as distinct from one dictated by others. The second condition of rational reflection on rules is one espoused by most believers in autonomy. To discuss whether it is essential to autonomy would involve discussing the intelligibility of romantic and existentialist alternatives, which is beyond the scope of this paper. For the purpose of this paper, however, it will be assumed to be a necessary condition of autonomy. The third possible condition, that of strength of will, seems to be much more contingently associated with autonomy, and will be ignored.

2   THE DEVELOPMENT OF THE FREE MAN

So much, then, for the different ways in which 'being free' can be understood. The lynch-pin of the analysis is the notion of man as a chooser, a rational being placed in what I have called the situation of practical reason. This is a presupposition of 'freedom' as a social principle; for a man who is 'not free' is one who has his options closed up in one way or other and this presupposes a being of whom it makes sense to say that he has options, i.e. that he is a chooser. In education, however, we are usually concerned with more than just preserving the capacity for choice; we are also concerned with the ideal of personal autonomy, which is a development of some of the potentialities inherent in the notion of man as a chooser. The concept of 'freedom' has now been sufficiently analysed to permit us to say a few things about the development of free men. Manifestly, in a paper of this length, there cannot be a massive marshalling of empirical studies which throw light on the conditions under which free men emerge. There is point, however, as will later be substantiated when something is said about the role of philosophy in the study of human learning, in giving an indication of the sorts of conditions that seem obviously relevant. For when we talk about the 'development' of free men we surely have in mind some process of learning, rather than some causal process such as is involved in the development of a photograph or of a plant. What, then, could be meant by 'learning' if it is suggested that human beings learn to become choosers or autonomous human beings?

There is a general concept of 'learning' used by most psychologists to draw attention to changes of behaviour that are not the product purely of maturation. I am not concerned with this general concept but only with the more specific one in which the changes in question are the result of past experience. At the centre of learning in this specific sense is some content that a learner makes his own by various processes of assimilation. He may copy it, grasp it, imitate it, memorise it and so on, depending on the type of content that it is. And what he can make his own depends largely on the existing state of his cognitive structure, 'structure' being understood as referring not just to what he has already assimilated in the way of content but also to how the content is conceived. For instance, for most of us so-called 'instrumental conditioning' operates only because we are capable of discerning a link between doing something and being rewarded, even though the link may be one of the extrinsic type referred to in the previous section. Similarly once a child has grasped the concept of a 'thing' he can quickly learn to recognise a variety of things such as bricks and balls by being presented with instances of them and having their features pointed out to him.

Now there are some concepts, such as that of 'thing' in the latter example of learning and 'means-to-an-end' in the former example; which are of particular importance in mental development in the theories of psychologists such as Piaget and Kohlberg, who have been much influenced by Kant. For they are categoreal concepts marking stages in the development of the human mind in that they define forms of human understanding and hence set limits to what can be learnt by imposing a framework for the assimilation of content. These fundamental types of concept, they argue, cannot therefore be taught by any process of direct instruction; rather they emerge as a result of the interaction between a mind equipped with potentialities for ordering and selecting and an environment which has invariant features which are there to discover. This kind of development, however, can be aided by what Kohlberg calls 'cognitive stimulation', which he contrasts with explicit instruction (see Kohlberg, 1968, 1969).

It is, surely, the learning of forms of understanding such as these (e.g., seeing something as a 'means to an end') rather than the assimilation of any particular content of experience that is crucial for the development of free men. Let me try to illustrate this contention briefly in the case of the development of the capacity for choice and in that of the achievement of autonomy.

(a) *Becoming a Chooser*

An account of becoming a chooser was sketched in section 1(a) by reference, mainly, to various forms of impairment in what were called, following Stanley Benn, 'subjective conditions'. But these themselves presuppose certain standing conditions without which they would be unintelligible. Being able to weigh up the pros and cons of alternatives and to act in the light of such deliberation presupposes that the individual can think in terms of taking means to an end. He appreciates, to a certain extent, the causal properties of things and can distinguish consequences brought about by his own agency from things that come about independently of his will. To do this he must possess the categoreal concepts of 'thinghood', 'causality', and 'means to an end'. These enable him to think 'realistically' in contradistinction to small children and paranoiacs whose consciousness is dominated by wishes and aversions. It presupposes, too, that he has a view of the world as an orderly system in which his confidence in his own powers and his expectations about the future will be confirmed. This is particularly important if his choice involves the delay of immediate gratification. Unlike the psychopath, the future is real to him and he has a steady disposition to take account of facts – both future and present. To regard himself as, to a certain extent, a determiner of his own destiny, which he must do if he is a chooser, he must have a sense of his own identity and that of others.

In developmental psychology there are two complementary approaches which throw light on these preconditions of choice. Piaget and his followers have mapped the stages at which this categoreal apparatus emerges; Freud and his followers, on the other hand, though allowing for the development of this apparatus in the doctrine of the 'ego', have concentrated more on the conditions under which it fails to emerge. They have shown the extent to which infantile, primary processes of thought persist in the mind of the adult and prevent it working rationally according to the principles dictated by this categoreal apparatus.

Piaget and Kohlberg, as has already been explained, argue that the development of this categoreal apparatus is the product, not of explicit teaching, but of cognitive stimulation. I will leave aside problematic Chomsky-type questions of the extent to which the emergence of this cognitive apparatus is innately determined; I will also leave aside the problems in the distinction made by Kohlberg between 'teaching' and 'cognitive stimulation'.[6] For, whatever allowance is made for other variables, the role of social influences which are connected with such 'stimulation' can be inferred from the fact that failure to develop such an apparatus has been shown by psychologists more interested in the Freudian type of approach, to be connected with certain types of socialisation or lack of it. Most pathological states can be described in terms of the absence of features of this apparatus and these defects can be correlated with typical conditions in early childhood. It is generally agreed, for instance, that psychopaths who live on their whims and impulses, for whom the future has little reality, and who have a way of thinking about the world rather like that of a young infant, are largely the product of homes which are rejecting towards the child and which provide a very inconsistent type of discipline.[7] Schizophrenics, whose belief-structure, especially in regard to their own identity, is deranged, are thought by some to be products of discrepant and irreconcilable attitudes towards them before they developed a secure sense of reality. They lack what Laing calls the 'ontological security' of a person who has developed the categoreal apparatus which is definitive of being a rational being or a chooser. As Laing puts it (1965, p. 39):

'Such a basically ontologically secure person will encounter all the hazards of life . . . from a centrally firm sense of his own and other people's reality and identity. It is often difficult for a person with such a sense of his integral selfhood and personal identity, of the permanency of things, of the reliability of natural processes, of the substantiality of others, to transpose himself into the world of an individual whose experiences may be utterly lacking in any unquestionable self-validating certainties.'

There is no need to multiply examples of failures to develop the apparatus necessary for becoming a chooser and to attempt to relate them to various types of defects in 'normal social conditions'. To do this thoroughly would necessitate writing a text-book on psychopathology. Of equal interest, however, from the point of view of educators, are cases of people who could be termed 'unreasonable' rather than 'irrational',[8] and whose way of life bears witness to the limited development of the capacities necessary for being a chooser, which again seem to be the product of a certain type of socialisation. An example of such a limited form of development is given by Josephine Klein in her book *Samples of English Culture* (1965). She singles out certain abilities which are presupposed in the account of being a chooser given in section 1(b) above. They are the ability to abstract and use generalisations, the ability to perceive the world as an ordered universe in which rational action is rewarded, the ability to plan ahead and to exercise self-control. She cites evidence from Luria and Bernstein to show that the extent to which these abilities develop depends on the prevalence of an elaborated form of language which is found in some strata of society but not in others. She also shows how the beliefs and conduct of some working-class sub-cultures are affected by the arbitrariness of their child-rearing techniques. Such happy-go-lucky people have a stunted capacity for choice because the future has only a limited relevance for them and because they are prejudiced, myopic and unreflective in their beliefs.[9]

So far examples have been given of the capacity for choice being impaired or stunted by others who, usually unwittingly, treat children in ways which bring about these results. It need hardly be added that these capacities can be neutralised, perhaps permanently impaired, by more conscious techniques which are combined together in brain-washing. The individual's categoreal apparatus can be attacked by making his environment as unpredictable as possible; his sense of time and place and of his own identity can be systematically undermined. He is gradually reduced to a state of acute anxiety, perhaps of mental breakdown, in which he is in a receptive state to being dominated by another who becomes the sole source of pleasure and security for him. He becomes suggestible and willing to accept beliefs, which, in his former life, he would have rejected out of hand. He becomes more or less a programmed man rather than a chooser. Domination by another can also take less dramatic and more temporary forms, as in some cases of being in love which in Freud's view belongs to the same family as being hypnotised. There are some people who sometimes find their way into the teaching profession, who seem to have this kind of hypnotic effect on others. These kinds of influence, which neutralise the capacity for choice, must be distinguished from others such as manipulation by bribing and threats, or feeding people with false information, which presuppose it. For these techniques rely on manipulation of the objective conditions of choice; they do not constitute an assault on the subjective conditions which are definitive of being a chooser.

It is not difficult to surmise why the most consistent finding from studies of child-rearing practices is that sensible children, who are capable of rational choice, seem to emerge from homes in which there is a warm attitude of acceptance towards children, together with a firm and consistent insistence on rules of behaviour without much in the way of punishment. An accepting attitude towards a child will tend to encourage trust in others and confidence in his own powers. A predictable social environment will provide the type of experience which is necessary for guiding behaviour by reflection on its consequences and so build up a belief in a future which is in part shaped by his own behaviour. Inconsistency in treatment, on the other hand, will encourage plumping rather than choosing and attachment to instant gratification; and a rejecting attitude will inhibit the development of the self-confidence which is necessary for being a chooser.

(b) *The Development of Autonomy*
It could well be that teachers should be much more mindful than they are of the possibility that many children come to them impaired or stunted in their capacity for choice, and that they should be more mindful of providing an environment which encourages it. In particular, perhaps, they should be chary of imposing a 'self-chosen curriculum' too quickly on children from homes in which there is little encouragement for children to be choosers. The fact is, however, that when teachers talk of 'freedom' as an educational ideal they usually have in mind the development of autonomy or self-regulation which is a far more ambitious ideal.

In thinking about a child's progress towards this ideal the work of

Piaget and Kohlberg, which is confirmed by that of Peck and Havighurst, is most illuminating. There is a general consensus that children pass through various stages in their conception of rules which is independent of the content of the rules concerned. They pass from regarding conformity to rules purely as a way of avoiding punishment and obtaining rewards to a level at which rules are regarded as entities in themselves that are just 'there' and which emanate from the collective will of the group and from people in authority. They finally pass to the level of autonomy, when they appreciate that rules are alterable, that they can be criticised and should be accepted or rejected on a basis of reciprocity and fairness.[10] The emergence of rational reflection about rules, which in section 1(c) was regarded as central to the Kantian conception of autonomy, is the main feature of the final level of moral development. Kohlberg produces cross-cultural evidence to support the general claim of the Piaget school, already mentioned, that these stages of development in the conception of rules are culturally invariant. He emphasises that the explanation of this is that the levels of conceiving of rules are in a hierarchical logical order; so there could be no other order in which development occurs. Though cultures differ in the content of rules, there is thus an invariant order in the way in which rules are conceived, although, of course, in many cultures there is no emergence to the autonomous stage.[11] Kohlberg makes the same claim about the limitations of teaching in this sphere as he makes with regard to the teaching of categories for thinking about the physical world such as causality and conservation. He argues that, though the content of rules is learnt by teaching or imitation, the form of conceiving of them is the product of interaction with the environment that can be accelerated or retarded by the amount of cognitive stimulation available.

Here again there are findings which emphasise the importance of the social environment, provided that we do not enter into niceties as to what is to be called 'teaching'. Kohlberg himself stresses the difference in rate and level of development towards autonomy of those who come from middle-class homes, in which there is plenty of 'cognitive stimulation'; and those who come from working-class homes. There is, too, a series of investigations by Bruner and his associates which are more far-reaching in their implications. He conducted experiments into ideas about conservation with the Wolof, a tribe in Senegal, and found that those who had not been exposed to Western influences embodied in schooling were unable to make distinctions such as that between how things are and how the individual views them. They had not the concept of different 'points of view'. He suggests that animistic thinking, in which individuals project their own agency into external nature, is the product of cultures in which attention is paid to satisfying the whims of individual children. Also the concept of conservation is achieved much earlier by the Tiv, who are encouraged to manipulate the external world, than by the Wolof who adopt a more passive attitude towards it. Bruner and Greenfield argue that amongst the Wolof the motor competence and manipulation of the individual is not encouraged. The child's personal desires and intentions, which might differentiate him from others, are not emphasised. What matters for them is the child's conformity to the group. Thus their concept of a child is of a being who starts off full of personal desires and intentions, but who has increasingly to subordinate such desires to the group. He thus becomes less and less of an individual because he is discouraged from thinking of himself as one. In cultures such as these, therefore, there is no encouragement for the individual to explore the world 'for himself' and find out what is true. What is true is what the group or the authority figure in the group says.[12]

We are, of course, familiar with this phenomenon in a less thorough-going form; for the appeal to the authority of the leader, parent, teacher or group, and the discouragement of individual testing out, is one of the main characteristics both of the second main developmental stage in the Piaget–Kohlberg theory and of traditionalist and collectivist types of society. But this attitude towards rules need not be just the product of vague social pressures and expectations; it can also be produced and perpetuated by the conscious techniques which we now call 'indoctrination'. For 'indoctrination' involves the passing on of fixed beliefs in a way which discourages questions about their validity. Societies, like the U.S.S.R., in which indoctrination is widespread, are not necessarily societies in which reasoning is altogether discouraged. They do not aim to undermine fundamentally people's capacities as choosers. The Russians are encouraged to calculate and to plan practical projects. Indeed they are renowned for their chess-playing and for their technology. What they are discouraged from doing is to question the validity of their moral and political beliefs and to place any emphasis on the role of the individual in determining his own destiny. They thus allow plenty of scope for the attitude to rules which is characteristic of Piaget's second stage but actively discourage any movement towards the autonomous stage, which they regard as an aberration of individualistic societies.

In the U.S.S.R. Makarenko achieved considerable success in dealing with delinquents by reliance mainly on group projects and on identification with the collective will of the community.[13] As presumably most of these delinquents were either at the first egocentric stage or suffering from various pathological conditions, it was a distinct sign of moral advancement for these individuals to function at the second level of morality at which the individual does the done thing, which is determined either by the group or by those in authority.

If Piaget and Kohlberg are right, however, in their assumptions about the logical sequence of stages in development of autonomy, *every* individual has to go through these stages of what Kohlberg calls 'good boy' and 'authority-oriented' morality before he can attain to the autonomous level. The Public Schools, who specialised in character-training, implicitly acknowledged this; for they combined an appeal to team spirit and to authority-based rule-conformity for all, with an emphasis on independence of mind and sticking to principles for those more senior boys who were singled out to command rather than simply to obey. It is questionable whether progressive educators have been sufficiently aware of the importance of this second level of development. They have, on the one hand, been reluctant for the staff to impose the rule of law but have been embarrassed by the fact that, if this is withdrawn, bullying and peer-group pressures take its place. On the other hand, they have emphasised the importance of individual choice without paying enough attention to the developmental stage which individual children have reached. Unless a child has been through the second level of morality, at which he is made to understand what an externally imposed rule is and to have some feeling about the inviolability of rules, it is dubious whether the notion of accepting or rejecting rules for himself is very meaningful to him. Decisions which are important in the shaping of character arise out of conflict situations. And how can a child go through any kind of existentialist agony if he is not acutely aware of the force of rules between which he has to choose?

So much, then, for general issues connected with the emergence to the autonomous stage of morality in so far as this involves rational reflection on rules. Some brief comments must now be made about the other aspect of autonomy which was thought to be essential to it when the notion was introduced in section 1(c) above, namely, authenticity.

For this aspect of autonomy to be operative, namely the proclivity of the individual to be moved by considerations intrinsic to the conduct concerned rather than just by extrinsic considerations such as rewards and punishment, approval and disapproval, two conditions have to be satisfied. First, the individual has to be sensitive to considerations which are to act as principles to back rules – e.g. to the suffering of others. Secondly, he has to be able, by reasoning, to view such considerations as reasons for doing some things rather than others. How individuals develop the required sensitivity is largely a matter of speculation. Obviously identification with others who already possess it is an operative factor; perhaps, too, a degree of first-hand experience is also necessary – e.g. not shielding young people but encouraging them to take part in practical tasks where there is suffering to be relieved. This kind of development can start very early; for Piaget and Kohlberg have shown not that children are incapable of such sensitivity when they are very young but that they are incapable of appealing to it as a backing for rules. In other words it does not function for them as a principle.

What then, can be done about encouraging the development of reasoning of this sort so that rules have the backing of authentically based principles? Presumably reasons for doing things can be indicated quite early on, even though it is appreciated that the child cannot yet think in this way. For unless there is this kind of 'cognitive stimulation' in the environment it is improbable that the child will emerge to the autonomous stage. Obviously an atmosphere of discussion and criticism, especially amongst children who are a bit older, will help to stimulate this development. Language, too, which approximates to what Bernstein calls an 'elaborated code', is very important in aiding this development as well as non-arbitrary methods of teaching rules.[14] I am not saying, of course, that any sane parent or teacher will, in the early stages, make a child's acceptance of the reasons a condition for his doing what is sensible. All I am saying is that rules can be presented in a non-arbitrary way *before* children are capable of accepting them for the reasons given, to help them to get to the stage when they follow rules because of the reasons for them. But it does not follow from this that, on many occasions, parents and teachers may not have to insist on certain forms of conduct even though the children do not accept the good sense of it. Indeed this is a common feature of the 'good boy' and 'rule-conformity' stages of morality.

3 THE INFLUENCE OF INSTITUTIONS

Kohlberg claims that, though the content of the morality of a particular community can be passed on by instruction and example, its form, which is defined by the way in which rules are conceived, cannot be so passed on. It is the product of interaction between the individual and his social environment which is merely assisted by 'cognitive stimulation'. How, then, if he is right, could an educational institution such as a secondary school, contribute to such development?

Obviously much can be done with regard to the appropriate *content* by instruction, example, and on the spot correction. In this boys and girls, who are a little more advanced in development, probably exert a more effective influence than the teachers themselves, as Thomas Arnold saw when he insisted that the older boys must bear the brunt of the responsibility for ensuring that rules of conduct are known and kept. But what about the form of morality, which is characterised by the prevailing attitude to rules? What can an educational institution contribute to this? Can it do much to aid development towards the autonomous stage?

No doubt much is contributed by a general atmosphere of discussion and by providing a backing of reasons for rules as well as insisting on them. A curriculum, too, which pays proper attention to those disciplines, such as literature and history, which provide a foundation for choice, is an obvious help. But of far-reaching importance, surely, is the general control system of the school and the motivational assumptions which support it. For Piaget's and Kohlberg's stages of development are 'writ large' in these all-pervasive features of the institution. It is, surely, unlikely that autonomy will be widely encouraged by an authoritarian system of control in which anything of importance is decided by the fiat of the headmaster and in which the prevailing assumption is that the appeal to a man is the only method of determining what is correct. Similarly in the motivational sphere of authenticity students are unlikely to develop a delight in doing things for reasons intrinsic to them if rewards and punishment, meted out both by the staff and by a fierce examination system, provide the stable incentives to the discipline of learning; for the institution itself embodies an attitude to conduct which is appropriate to Piaget's first stage of development. These institutional realities are bound to structure the perceptions of the students. If an institution embodies an attitude to rules that is characteristic of an earlier stage of development, teachers who attempt to encourage a more developed attitude have an uphill task; for in their attempts at 'cognitive stimulation' they are working against the deadening directives of the institution.

The inference to be drawn from this is not that every school, which upholds an ideal of autonomy, should straightaway abolish its punishment and examination systems and introduce a school parliament which should direct the affairs of the institution in a way which is acceptable to autonomous men. Apart from the rational objections to the possibility of educational institutions being purely 'democratic'[15] it ignores the implications to be drawn from the Piaget–Kohlberg theory. For on this view children have to pass from seeing rules as connected with punishments and rewards to seeing them as ways of maintaining a gang-given or authoritatively ordained rule structure before they can adopt a more autonomous attitude towards them. Kohlberg has shown that many adolescents are still only at the first 'pre-moral' level; so the suggestion that an institution should be devised for them which is structured only in terms of the final stage is grossly inappropriate. Progressive schools, therefore, which insist *from the start* on children making their own decisions and running their own affairs, ignore the crucial role which the stage of conventional morality plays in moral development. The more enlightened ones in fact have a firm authority structure for the school which is arranged so that increasing areas of discretion and participation in decision-making are opened up for the older pupils. This attempt to arrange an institution so that its control system is not out of tune with stages of development seems eminently sensible. In fact the Public Schools, at their best, have approximated to this. They have combined a great emphasis on decency, doing the done thing, and respect for authority with a pressure on prefects to develop some degree of autonomy. The criticism of this system is that the emphasis on a second-level type of regulation was overdone and that third-level type of morality was encouraged only for the few who were singled out for positions of eminence.

It might, finally, be tentatively suggested that, though there are stages in character development which are 'writ large' in systems of institutional control, the arrangement is a hierarchical one. Earlier stages are not completely superseded; rather they are, ideally speaking, caught up in and transformed by the next stage. When a system maintained purely by naked force and the dispensation of rewards gives way to a system dependent on the belief in the sanctity of rules enshrined in tradition or laid down by authority, force and rewards are not abandoned. Rather they are placed in the background as palpable supports for the authority structure, which have to be employed if the support appropriate to an authority system becomes ineffective. Similarly when, with the advent of individualism and the belief in reason, traditional systems are challenged, and fundamental questions are asked about the institution of authority itself, authority becomes rationalised, not superseded. Its structure is adapted to the reasons for having it, people are appointed to positions of authority on relevant grounds, and their spheres of competence are carefully defined.

In a similar way the autonomous man is not a person who operates only at the level of a principled morality. He is not impervious to the promise of reward and punishment; he does many things because it is the decent thing to do or because they have been laid down by authority; but he is capable both of doing the same things because he sees their point as flowing from his fundamental principles, and of challenging certain forms of conduct that are laid down and acting differently because of his own convictions. He has, in other words, a rational attitude both to tradition and to authority. My guess is, however, that much of the conduct of autonomous people is governed by a second-level type of morality. They refrain from stealing and incest, because they do not regard it as the thing to do. They pay their debts, keep their promises, and adopt the principle of first come first served when queuing for goods in short supply, without pondering much on the principles involved. Maybe they have thought about the ethics of such practices; maybe they are in part moved by considerations connected with their principles. But my guess is that they carry with them a solid precipitate from the conventional stage of morality whose motivation sustains the more mundane levels of their conduct. For unless a person has been solidly bedded down in this stage of morality he will not have the basic experience of rules as regulators of his impulses and as checks on the more calculating type of hedonism, deriving from the first level of morality. This provides a proper preparation for the autonomous stage of morality, and the attitude to rules remains with him even though the more rational attitude to rules, appropriate to the autonomous stage, is superimposed on it.

4 ASSUMPTIONS ABOUT LEARNING

Throughout this over-ambitious paper I have referred to various studies by psychologists and have indulged in what seem to be speculative sorties into the empirical which have sometimes been prefaced by remarks such as 'My guess is'. What justification has a philosopher for behaving like this, even though he is a philosopher of education and therefore necessarily has his ear closer to the ground than his less mundane colleagues in philosophy departments?

I could deploy a general thesis about the nature of philosophy to justify this procedure, in which I would try to show that the dividing line between philosophy and first-order activities, such as science and morality, is not as easy to draw as many have thought. But there is no need, in this case, to appeal to such general considerations; for the justification lies in the nature of human learning, which, as I shall try very briefly to indicate, permits observations of this quasi-empirical character to be made.

In ordinary straightforward cases of human learning, in which some content is understood, memorised, imitated or made a person's own in various other ways, there is a sense in which the concept of 'learning' is neither monolithic nor concerned with anything that requires empirical investigation. For it draws attention to a range of achievements which are diverse and whose different criteria dictate the sort of thing that must be done if learning is to take place. Suppose, for instance, that one learns, in biology, what mammals are. 'Learns' here picks out the achievement of being able to classify animals in a certain way. The achievement involves being able to relate 'mammal' to other concepts such as 'mammarian glands' and to recognise cases of mammals. The so-called processes of learning involve being put in the way of both features of what it means to grasp the concept of 'mammal'. Examples are pointed out and the features which they have in common are explained. Learning a skill is different; for this involves, in the case of bodily skills like swinging a golf-club, the co-ordination of movements in a certain pattern. But here the relevant type of mastery dictates what learning must be like; for how else could such a pattern of movements be developed except by some kind of practice in moving the body in this way? Remembering similarly must involve some content which is accurately reproduced; so learning in this sphere must involve devices by means of which accuracy in reproduction is ensured. The type of achievement determines the general form of the process of learning.

This fundamental point about the concept of learning makes clear why the philosophy is intimately concerned with it; for it is a philosopher's task to explicate in general what is meant by 'understanding', 'knowing how to do things', 'remembering', etc. Anything that is to count as 'learning' in these spheres must be related intelligibly in some way to the achievement in question. By this I mean that there must be some relationship such as that of being logically presupposed to, or conceptually connected with, the achievement in question. Of course, the philosopher may not know all the *details* of the achievement. He may be rusty on his mathematics or ignorant about golf. But the details will be supplied not by empirical psychologists but by those who know a lot about the structure of the forms of understanding or skills in question. There are, of course, important empirical questions about aids to learning such as the influence of repetition; there are empirical questions about individual differences and about conditions which militate against learning. But the central core of what we call 'learning' depends upon making explicit criteria of 'match' and intelligibility of content in the various achievements of which human beings are capable.

In this paper, however, I have not dwelt at all on the learning of the *contents* of various forms of achievement. Rather I have been concerned with the development of forms of understanding, characterising both a chooser and an autonomous person. In suggesting, for instance, that to become autonomous what is necessary is a predictable social environment, encouragement of the individual's attempts to manipulate things, and a general conviction that an individual's point of view matters, I have, in effect, been citing conditions that make the development of various components in the concept of 'choosing' intelligible. Brainwashing was explained as a process that undermines the categoreal apparatus necessary for choice by depriving the individual of a temporal framework and of a sense of his own identity. Similarly indoctrination was represented as a process that drastically discourages the fundamental questioning of the validity of rules which characterises the autonomous stage. Unreasonable people were seen to be the product of a social environment embodying arbitrariness and a language that is concrete and weak on a syntax that aids thought in terms of universals. It was suggested that it is difficult to develop autonomy in an institution that is structured in terms of appeals to authority or in which rewards and punishments are the main incentives to learning. For it is such all-pervasive procedures that determine how an individual is likely to structure his experience. In proceeding in this way I am only sketching in some of the conditions of 'cognitive stimulation', which, on Kohlberg's view, encourage development from stage to stage or other influences that fixate people at a certain stage of development.

The question must be asked, however, whether in providing this kind of social setting for Kohlberg's speculations I am doing anything for which a philosopher is specially suited. There are parts of it, surely, which are eminently the concern of the philosopher. Piaget's and Kohlberg's basic claim is that the order of development of stage concepts is culturally invariant because it is based on logical relationships between levels of conceiving. If this is correct it has manifest importance in the moral sphere. It would dictate, for instance, the rather cautious conservatism in moral education set out in section 3. For the purpose of this article I have assumed it to be a tenable view. But elsewhere[16] I have questioned it at least on the ground that Kohlberg has not clearly spelt out the logical connections.

Secondly it is a philosophical task to break down a notion like that of autonomy and to point out that some process of learning is required in relation to each aspect of the achievement of autonomy. This fits in with the general account of the philosopher's role in relation to learning set out at the beginning of this section. So does the attempt to indicate the *sort* of conditions under which forms of conception could be intelligibly learnt. For with these, as with any other concepts, one has to postulate both conditions in which they could be applied and some aids to conceptualisation, even if they take the form of 'cognitive stimulation' rather than of direct instruction. It is an empirical question, of course, to determine the conditions which actually *do* have a marked influence. For instance, in the case of learning perceptual concepts of the sort that are involved in geometry – e.g. square, round – it is a philosophical point that some kind of experience is necessary for learning the concepts; for otherwise how could the concept be *applied*, which is part of our understanding of what it means to have learnt a concept? But it may be an empirical fact that a lot of manipulatory and visual experience is a great help in learning. This may not be the case with practical concepts such as that of 'toy' or 'tool'. And with the types of concept that are crucial in the development of autonomy, the case of the Wolof, studied by Bruner and Greenfield, suggests that both exploratory experiences and social influences are very important.

There are, of course, other discoveries in the developmental sphere about which the philosopher could have little to say – e.g. the importance attached to sexual and aggressive wishes in the Freudian explanation of why people do not develop along Piagetian lines and learn ways of interpreting things that lead to various forms of irrationality which even sometimes prevent them from achieving the status of choosers (see section 1(b)). But in these types of explanation, as well as in the types of explanation which have been used to account for the influence of institutions and social conditions, there are present some all-pervasive assumptions about generalisation in learning, whose status is somewhat obscure. What is to be made, for instance, of assumptions such as:

'If human beings are exposed to a highly unpredictable environment, they will tend to lack confidence in their ability to predict and control events.'

'If children are actively discouraged from asking questions they will acquire habits of unquestioning acceptance.'

Assumptions such as these proliferate in the literature of psychology in general as well as in the particular speculations in which I have indulged in parts of this paper. All of them could be falsified in particular cases, though all of them have a kind of intuitive plausibility about them. Their plausibility derives from the fact that they all manifestly satisfy the basic condition of all human learning, namely that of an intelligible connection between what is learnt and the conditions of learning. It is not the philosopher's task to explore the extent to which these common-sense assumptions are true. But philosophical points can be made about the types of condition which must be satisfied for different types of learning to take place. Assumptions such as these manifestly satisfy such conditions. We are, I think, only at the beginning of our understanding of what is a philosophical point about learning and what is an empirical point. This distinction applies to the content of experience as well as to its form, though I have mainly been concerned with the latter in this paper. It would, however, take another paper to begin to get to grips with this central problem in the philosophy of education. I have only introduced it briefly at the end of this one in order to defend myself against the charge that, because I have referred to things that go on in the world, I am necessarily bringing the Owl of Minerva down to the level of the cuckoo in the nest.

REFERENCES

1. I wish to express my thanks to colleagues whose comments helped me to improve this paper – especially Stanley Benn and Geoffrey Mortimore of the Australian National University and Mrs P. A. White of the University of London Institute of Education.
2. Especially in Stanley Benn's paper on 'Conditions of Autonomy', which he read to a conference of the AAP in 1969 and which I discussed with him at length during my period as Visiting Fellow at the Australian National University. This paper was itself a development of ideas worked out, between Stanley Benn and W. Weinstein in their 1971 paper 'Being Free to Act, and Being a Free Man'.

3. For development of such points see Peters, 1966, Ch. VII.
4. See ibid., Chs III, IV, V, VII esp.
5. See Peters (1964, 1971a).
6. See Peters (1971b).
7. See, for instance, Peck and Havighurst (1960), pp. 109–11.
8. For distinction see Peters (1971a).
9. See Klein (1965).
10. Kohlberg actually breaks Piaget's three stages up into six stages with three levels. But it would be out of place to pursue these refinements.
11. See Kohlberg (1968, 1969).
12. See Greenfield and Bruner (1969).
13. See Lilge (1958), esp. pp. 25–6.
14. See Bernstein (1961, 1969).
15. See Hirst and Peters (1970), Ch. 7.
16. See Peters (1971b).

BIBLIOGRAPHY

Benn, S. I. and Weinstein, W., 'Being Free to Act, and Being a Free Man', *Mind*, Vol. LXXX (1971), pp. 194–211.

Bernstein, B. B., 'Social Class and Linguistic Development: a Theory of Social Learning', in Halsey, A. H., Floud, J. and Anderson, C. A., *Education, Economy and Society* (New York: Free Press, 1961).

Bernstein, B. and Henderson, D., 'Social Class Differences in the Relevance of Language to Socialisation', *Sociology*, Vol. 3 (1969).

Greenfield, P. M. and Bruner, J. S., 'Culture and Cognitive Growth', in Goslin, D. A., *Handbook of Socialisation: Theory and Research* (Chicago: Rand McNally, 1969).

Hirst, P. H. and Peters, R. S., *The Logic of Education* (Routledge & Kegan Paul, 1970).

Klein, J., *Samples of English Culture*, 2 vols (Routledge & Kegan Paul, 1965).

Kohlberg, L., 'Early Education: a Cognitive Developmental View', *Child Development*, Vol. 31 (1968).

Kohlberg, L., 'Stage and Sequence: the Cognitive Developmental Approach to Socialization', in Goslin, D. A. (Ed.), *Handbook of Socialization: Theory and Research* (Chicago: Rand McNally, 1969).

Laing, R. D., *The Divided Self* (Penguin Books, 1965).

Lilge, F., *Anton Semyonovitch Makarenko* (Berkeley and Los Angeles: University of California Press, 1958).

Peck, R. F. and Havighurst, R. J., *The Psychology of Character Development* (New York, John Wiley, 1960).

Peters, R. S., 'Mental Health as an Educational Aim', in Hollins, T. H. B. (Ed.), *Aims of Education: the Philosophical Approach* (Manchester University Press, 1964).

Peters, R. S., *Ethics and Education* (Allen & Unwin, 1966).

Peters, R. S., 'Education and Human Development', in Selleck, R. W. (Ed.), *Melbourne Studies in Education* (Melbourne University Press, 1970).

Peters, R. S., 'Reason and Passion', in Vesey, G. (Ed.), *The Proper Study*, Vol. 4, Royal Institute of Philosophy (Macmillan, 1971a).

Peters, R. S., 'Moral Development: a Plea for Pluralism', in Mischel, T. (Ed.), *Cognitive Development and Epistemology* (New York: Academic Press, 1971b).

Chapter 7

Moral Development and Moral Learning[*][1]

INTRODUCTION

The most obvious way in which a philosopher can contribute to work
on moral education is through work in ethics. Just as work in
mathematical or scientific education could not get off the ground
without a determinate idea of the structure of what has to be learnt
in these spheres, so too a determinate notion of 'morality' is an
essential precondition for any serious approach to moral education.
It might be argued, too, that it is particularly important for philosophers to do this because of the covert way in which ethical assumptions are smuggled into empirical work in this field. Any psychological account of moral development or moral education must be
from a particular standpoint in ethics; for the delimitation of 'moral'
is not a neutral matter. Psychologists working within Piagetian,
Freudian, or social learning frameworks are too apt to work with an
implicit ethical position. The job of the philosopher is, therefore, to
make such ethical positions explicit and to discuss the arguments that
might be given for them.

I have done some work previously along these lines[2] and do not
want, in this paper, to go over that kind of ground again in any
detailed way. Instead I propose to explore another range of issues
which are equally appropriate for a philosopher of education. These
are issues about types of learning. It might be objected straight away
that these are empirical issues about which a philosopher could have
little to say. But this is not true. Processes of learning and of development are processes through which a variety of abilities and achieve-

* Reprinted, with the permission of the editor, from *The Monist*, Vol. 58, No. 4
(October 1974).

ments are mastered. These are very diverse. People come to understand, to remember, to make inferences; they master skills and develop attitudes. Learning, as distinct from maturation, involves coming up to the mark, according to the different criteria involved in these achievements, as a result of experience. There must therefore be some intelligible connection between the achievements concerned and the experiences through which a person comes up to the mark. It would be unintelligible, for instance, that a person could attain a mastery of Euclid by just standing on his head – unless, that is, a special story was told about the connection between adopting this position and grasping relationships between angles, straight lines, etc. For, if Euclid is to be understood, there must be experiences in which attention is paid to features of figures such as triangles and squares. In a similar way it is not purely an empirical point that practice in moving the body in certain ways is indispensable for mastering a skill like swinging a golf club. In every case of human learning the relevant type of mastery dictates the general character of the learning experiences. There are empirical questions about which *particular* learning experiences, taken from a range of possible ones, in fact tend to promote the desired achievements most effectively. But the central core of 'learning' depends upon some kind of match between the learning processes and the desired achievements. So analysis by philosophers of these achievements is very important.

In breaking down particular subjects for learning, as in programmed learning for instance, the work of the specialist who knows about the structure of what has to be learnt is much more central than that of the empirical psychologist who knows about *general* conditions of learning, such as the influence of repetition, rest-pauses and incentives. The subject specialist, too, would be wise to have a philosopher at his elbow, if he himself has not developed this way of thinking. Otherwise a conception of a subject may be developed, as in the new mathematics, and the content carefully structured, without adequate realisation of the presuppositions about the nature of the subject which the programme of study embodies. This is true of all subjects – e.g. science, art, music, history, religion, social studies, etc., though too dimly appreciated. Unfortunately the 'philosophies of' the various subjects taught in schools, and their relevance for how the subjects are taught, are the most undeveloped area of the philosophy of education.

Now morality is not a subject on the curriculum of most schools – at least in the sense in which mathematics is. And the only specialists in its structure are moral philosophers. It is often said, too, that willy-nilly every teacher is a teacher of morals. So, whether or not programmes of moral education are introduced more explicitly into the classroom, there is an obvious case for getting a bit clearer about the achievements involved and hence the sorts of learning experiences that people must go through if they are to emerge as moral beings from their childhood. This will enable evidence produced by psychologists to be looked at with a more discriminating eye. For often evidence which is produced for confirming a particular theory in psychology does not necessarily refute another theory. For the different theories may be concerned with different aspects of moral learning or moral development, or with a different conception of what is central to morality.

It is assumed that there is a conflict between different psychological theories of moral development. Instruction-based teachers and Skinnerians are insistent on the success of their methods in moral learning as in any other form of learning. The advocates of experience and discovery are equally enthusiastic about their methods, and with encouragement from their reading of Piaget and Kohlberg, have moved into the moral sphere. And those with a more Freudian type of ancestry still stick doggedly to their belief in the role of identification and guilt. Is it possible to reconcile these seemingly discordant voices about what matters in moral education? Perhaps – but to attempt such a reconciliation I must briefly outline the standpoint about morality from which I approach these different theories of moral development. I propose to confine it to the area of morals that is concerned with interpersonal rules.

1 RATIONAL MORALITY

It is often suggested nowadays that the only alternatives open to people in the moral position that they may adopt are either the relics of some traditional code or some version of a subjectivist stance such as Existentialism or a 'situational ethic'.[3] But these, surely, are not the only alternatives open. There is a middle way between tradition and some sort of romantic protest. This middle way is closely connected with the use of reason. This enables people to adopt a critical attitude towards what has been established. They may accept it or reject it on its merits. But in so doing they need not take up a purely subjective stance. It is significant, for instance, that young people, who are very critical of what their elders do, criticise it in terms of the injustice, exploitation or suffering brought about by adult mismanagement. They are united in assuming that this line of criticism is pertinent; they do not just voice private objections to the plight of coloured people, to the selectiveness of the educational system, or to the paternalism of their teachers.

In order to make clear what is meant by the use of reason in morality it is important to make a distinction between the form and content of the moral consciousness. This distinction is similar to that which can be made in the sphere of beliefs about the world. The content of a belief might be that the earth is round. But this belief could be held in different ways. It could be believed just because it had been read in a book or proclaimed by an authority. On the other hand it could be believed because someone had examined it, had viewed it critically and looked into the evidence for it, like a scientist. Thus a belief with the same content could be held in quite different ways, which would constitute two distinct forms which the belief might have. Similarly in morals someone could believe that gambling was wrong simply because his parents had brought him up to believe it. On the other hand he might have reflected on the practice of gambling and might have decided that it was wrong because of the suffering brought about by the practice.

Holding beliefs rationally is to adopt one possible form for beliefs. It is possible, therefore, that people could share a certain content of beliefs which had a different form. An unreflective peasant and a philosopher, for instance, might both believe that it is wrong to break promises. Alternatively people might look at beliefs in the same sort of way but disagree with regard to content because they gave different weight to considerations relevant to holding them. Reflective people, for instance, after due thought, might disagree about the ethics of abortion, even though they both accepted the relevance of the considerations advanced on either side. This type of distinction is very pertinent when discussing morals or moral education. For too much weight may be given to consensus or to lack of it without considering whether the consensus relates to content or to form.

My interest, needless to say, is in the emergence of a rational form of morality, which enables a person to adopt a stance that is critical of tradition but not subjective. But this cannot be characterised purely in terms of the *ability* to reason, in the sense of making inferences, as I have argued elsewhere.[4] To start with, if this ability is to be effectively exercised, it must be supported by a group of rational passions connected with the demands for consistency, order, clarity and relevance. Secondly, if this is to be exercised in the sphere of inter-personal conduct the individual must be capable of what Piaget calls reversibility in thought. He must be able to look at rules and practices from other people's point of view. And, unless we are going to postulate a society of rational egoists, we must also assume on the part of those with a capacity for reasoning, a *concern* for the interests of others as well as for their own interests. For what sort of point could reasoning about conduct have unless there were some concern to ameliorate the human predicament, to consider people's interests? In other words I am adopting a position in morals similar to that of David Hume who argued for some kind of shared response amongst human beings, connected with sympathy, which he at times called the 'sentiment for humanity'. Perhaps neither concern for others, nor concern for oneself, can be demonstrated as necessary for the application of reasoning to interpersonal conduct. But I am assuming them as preconditions in my system of rational morality.

Other principles must also be presupposed if it is assumed that interpersonal rules of conduct are to be discussed by rational beings with a concern for people's interests. For, as one of the main features of the use of reason is the settling of issues on *relevant* grounds – i.e. the banning of arbitrariness, some kind of impartiality with regard to people's claims is also required. They cannot be ignored just because of the colour of their eyes, or ruled out of court just because of the colour of their skin. People must be treated with respect as sources of arguments and claims. Without too, the general presumption that people should tell the truth rational discussion would be impossible; for, as a general practice, systematic lying would be counter-productive in relation to any common concern to discover what ought to be done. Finally, too, there must be some presumption in favour of freedom. For without freedom of speech, the community would be hamstrung in relation to its concern to arrive at an answer; for even the most offensive or simple members might have something of importance to contribute. There must also be a presumption in favour of freedom of action; for what rational man would seriously discuss what ought to be done without also demanding freedom to do it?

These fundamental principles do not, of course, lay down in detail what ought to be done. They do not, in other words, provide any detailed *content* to the moral life. Rather they supply a *form* for the moral consciousness; they sensitise us to what is relevant when we think about what is right and wrong. But neither do the principles underlying science guarantee an agreed content for a science. In both cases all that is provided is a form of thought which structures experience. In the scientific case assumptions about the world are systematically submitted to discussion and to observational tests.

Some are discarded and others survive as the current content of scientific knowledge. Similarly in the moral case, when current codes are reflected on in the light of such principles, as happened in the seventeenth century when reflective lawyers such as Grotius tried to agree upon laws of the sea against piracy, it comes to be seen that the content of codes are not all of equal importance. There are some types of basic rules – e.g. concerning contracts, the care of the young and property – which can be seen to be necessary to any continuing form of social life in which the human condition is going to be tolerable at all, man being what he is and the conditions of life on earth being what they are.[5] But other rules are much more dependent on local economic and geographical conditions such as prohibitions on usury, birth-control and possessiveness. Stability and consensus at a basic level are quite compatible with change and experiment at other levels. And these differences in stability of content can be determined by reasons deriving from fundamental principles such as fairness and the consideration of people's interests.

Actually disagreement over content between reflective people can be greatly exaggerated. Is there widespread disagreement between reflective people over what I have called basic rules? But, from the point of view of rational morality, it is more crucial to ask whether or not, in determining any particular content, people do or do not accept as relevant more or less similar considerations, even though they give differing *weight* to them?[6] In discussing sexual matters, for instance, is not the harm done to children by being fatherless thought morally relevant, or the lack of respect for persons evident in some forms of prostitution both within and outside marriage? In considering the breaking of contracts is not the lack of truthfulness, as well as the unhappiness caused, thought to be relevant? In discussing the merits of gambling do we ever dwell approvingly or disapprovingly on the amount of greenness in the world brought about by the construction of card-tables? If we think a man wicked is it normally by virtue of his height? Maybe we do not always arrive at the same conclusion about what is right and wrong, about the content of morality. But is not the form of thought of reflective people about it structured in terms of shared principles which make considerations relevant?

2 FORM AND CONTENT IN MORAL DEVELOPMENT AND LEARNING

The distinction which I have made between form and content in presenting a thumb-nail sketch of the structure of a rational morality is also extremely relevant to accounts of moral development and moral learning. This distinction is explicitly made by Lawrence Kohlberg in his account of moral development.[7] But as he is interested only in the development of the form of experience rather than in the learning of content there is a one-sided emphasis in his theory. Kohlberg admits that the content of rules – e.g. about honesty, punctuality, tidiness – is learnt by instruction and imitation, aided by rewards and punishment, praise and blame. But he is not interested in such habit formation; for he claims that such habits are short term and situation specific. They are of minor importance in moral development which depends on how rules are conceived rather than on cultural content. There is a transition from conceiving of rules as connected with rewards and punishments to conceiving of them as 'out there' backed by praise and blame from the peer-group and authority figures, and finally to conceiving of them as alterable conventions depending upon consent and reciprocity. Development depends not upon explicit teaching, backed by reinforcement, but upon the interaction of the child with his social environment, which is aided or retarded by the amount of 'cognitive stimulation' available to the child which helps him to conceive of the social environment in the required manner.

The relevance of Kohlberg's theory for the development of a rational form of morality is obvious enough; for that is what he is talking about. Like Piaget, whom he follows, he is a Kantian. But in contrasting the interaction with the environment, which stimulates the development of a rational form of morality, with 'teaching', which he thinks is singularly ineffective in this sphere, he makes it look too much as if the child, as it were, does it himself. This Dewey-like impression has to be corrected by a closer look at the sorts of influence that constitute 'cognitive stimulation'. But there are also, on this theory, most interesting implications for the learning of content, in which Kohlberg evinces little interest. For the form of the child's morality, defined by his conception of the rules which are constitutive of its content, on Kohlberg's theory determines both the type of content that can be assimilated and the aids which are available for this assimilation. In other words the type of 'reinforcement' used by Skinnerians can be shown to be peculiarly appropriate to learning specific types of *content* at certain stages of development. If it is important that the child should internalise a certain type of content – e.g. rules about not stealing – there may only be certain ways in which this can be done at a certain age – e.g. by being rewarded or praised for conformity. So Skinnerians may be right about the learning of content. But learning the *form* of experience may be a very different matter. And some methods of teaching content might impede the child from developing to a stage at which a different conception of rules is possible.

My argument will be, therefore, not just that Kohlberg's account of the development of a rational form of morality is compatible with a Skinnerian type of account of the learning of content in early childhood; for it is more than compatible in that it provides conceptual levels which define the types of 'reinforcement' and instruction that are possible. I shall argue, in addition, that no adequate account can be given of the development of a rational form of morality without more attention to the learning of content than Kohlberg is disposed to give. Furthermore I shall indicate that there are certain ways in which content may be learnt which actively impede the development of a rational form of morality. I will defend this thesis by considering briefly Kohlberg's thesis about stages of development with particular attention to the types of 'cognitive stimulation' that may be necessary. I will then pass to deploying my thesis about the importance of the learning of content.

In making suggestions about development and learning in these spheres I will adopt the strategy implied by my brief remarks about the relationship between the logical and psychological aspects of learning in section 1. I will indicate some of the relevant achievements as I proceed and cite empirical evidence in so far as it relates to learning experiences relevant to such achievements.

3 THE DEVELOPMENT OF A RATIONAL FORM OF MORALITY

(a) *The Egocentric Stage*

The first significant stage in moral development, on the Piaget–Kohlberg theory, is that in which the child has an egocentric conception of rules. He does what is laid down because he wants to avoid punishment or to obtain rewards. This is not regarded as a primitive instrumental conditioning type of situation in which some response is reinforced and gradually stamped in without the individual seeing any connection between what he does and the state of affairs, whether pleasant or painful, which results. Rather the child is envisaged as seeing the means–end type of connection involved. For this stage to have been reached the child must have developed a basic cognitive and affective apparatus; he is no longer an infant beset by various forms of pre-rational wishes and aversions. He must be able to delay gratification and to plan his behaviour to a limited extent. This form of commerce with the world and with others as sources of pain or gratification presupposes the development of a primitive type of categoreal apparatus with which Piaget, following Kant, was very much concerned in his account of what he called the Copernican revolution of early childhood.[8] If the child is to think in terms of taking means to an end he must appreciate, to a certain extent, the causal properties of things and must be able to distinguish consequences brought about by his own agency from those that come about independently of his will. He must possess the categoreal concepts of 'thinghood' and 'causality' in a primitive form. He must have some kind of framework of time and space. He must be able to distinguish himself from others. These categoreal concepts define the development of what Freud called the ego, and reality thinking.[9]

What assumptions have to be made about the sorts of experiences which are likely to lead to this sort of development? Obviously, to start with, the child will have to be provided with plenty of opportunities for the manipulation of things. The more controversial issue is the role of adults and other children in bringing about this early development. Now followers of Piaget have been most active in demonstrating that this framework of concepts, necessary for rational thought and choice, cannot be imparted by specific teaching. The child has to be provided with plenty of concrete experience. He will gradually come to grasp these organising notions if he is suitably stimulated like the slave in *Meno*. And there is a sense in which these contentions *must* be true. For what is being learnt is a principle, which provides unity to a number of previously disconnected experiences. This has to be 'seen' or grasped by the individual and it cannot be grasped as a principle unless the individual is provided with experience of the items which it unifies. If information is being imparted, which has to be memorised, the teacher can instruct the learner explicitly in what has to be learnt; in learning a skill the particular movements can be demonstrated explicitly for the learner to copy or practice. But, if the teacher is trying to get the learner to grasp a principle, all he can do is to draw attention to common features of cases and hope that the penny will drop. Also once the child has grasped the principle, he knows how to go on, as Wittgenstein puts it; there is thus no limit to the number of cases that he will see as falling under the principle. There is a sense, therefore, in which the learner gets out much more than any teacher could have put in. Kohlberg's objection to *specific* teaching is therefore readily explained; for principles just are not the sorts of things that can be applied only to a specific number of items which could be imparted by a teacher.

Kohlberg, of course, is using 'teaching' in a very narrow sense to mean something like 'explicit instruction'. It is only this very narrow conception of 'teaching' which can be properly contrasted with 'cognitive stimulation'; for most people would say that Socrates was teaching the slave in *Meno* even though he was not explicitly telling him things.

The learning situation, however, can be influenced by adults in much more subtle ways. There is evidence to suggest, for instance, that these concepts develop much more slowly if the child is actively discouraged from exploring and manipulating the physical environment.[10] If the child, too, is to do what is demanded of him attention is required. Now fear of punishment for not doing what is demanded is more likely to distract attention than the prospect of a reward. All the evidence confirms this assumption; for positive reinforcement is generally accepted by psychologists as being much more conducive to learning than negative reinforcement.

There is also the negative type of evidence provided by pathological studies; for most pathological states can be described in terms of the absence of features of this categoreal structure, and these defects can often be correlated with typical conditions in early childhood. It is generally agreed, for instance, that psychopaths, who live on their whims and impulses, for whom the future has little reality, are largely the product of homes which are rejecting towards the child and which provide a very inconsistent type of discipline.[11] Similarly schizophrenics, whose belief structure in regard to their own identity, and to that of the permanence of objects and the reliability of causal processes in the physical world, is deranged, are thought by some to be products of discrepant and irreconcilable attitudes towards them before they could develop a secure sense of reality.[12]

Further evidence of the importance of such general social influences on the early development of the preconditions for a rational form of morality can be found in sociological studies of people who might be termed unreasonable rather than irrational.[13] Josephine Klein, for instance, singles out certain abilities which are important in the development of reasoning – the ability to abstract and use generalisations, the ability to perceive the world as an ordered universe in which rational action is rewarded, the ability to plan ahead and control gratification. She cites evidence from Luria and Bernstein to show that the *extent* to which these abilities develop depends upon the prevalence of an elaborated form of language which is found in some strata of society but not in others. She also shows how the belief and conduct of some working-class sub-cultures are affected by the arbitrariness of their child-rearing techniques.[14]

In brief, the empirical evidence supports the logical analysis of the learning situation. If a child has to develop a basic apparatus for conceiving of an orderly world in which concepts such as those of 'thing' and 'causality' are firmly planted, he has to be given plenty of experience of objects and processes instantiating such concepts. If he is to learn to plan and to control gratification he must also live in a social world which provides regularities for him which will enable him to predict and to enjoy satisfying consequences of his actions. And so on. It is not difficult, therefore, to surmise why the most consistent findings from studies of child-rearing practices are that sensible children, who are capable of reasoning later on, emerge from homes in which there is a warm attitude of acceptance towards children, together with a firm and consistent insistence on rules without much in the way of punishment. An accepting attitude will tend to encourage trust in others and confidence in the individual's own powers. A predictable social environment will provide the type of experience which is necessary for guiding behaviour by reflection on its consequences and so build up a belief in a future which is, in part, shaped by his own decisions. Inconsistency in treatment, on the other hand, will encourage plumping rather than reflective choice, and attachment to instant gratification. A rejecting attitude will inhibit the development of self-confidence and techniques of punishment will generate anxiety and will provide conditions which are too distracting for much learning to take place.

These social influences may be spoken of as forms of 'cognitive stimulation'. For their function is to provide conditions in which rational capacities can begin to develop. But these influences provide a type of social environment for which adults are largely responsible. A contrast should not, therefore, be made between 'cognitive stimulation' and 'teaching' of a sort that suggests that adult influence is not of central importance to both. There is a danger in soft-pedalling the role of instruction in moral development. For people often go to the other extreme and assume that children must be left alone to find it all out for themselves. But they will not develop in this way, as in discovery methods generally, unless adults provide a structured and supportive type of social environment.

(b) *Rule-following*

At the first level of development the child, as I have explained, is acquiring the general apparatus for reasoning. But his attitude is basically egocentric; he sees conformity with them basically as a way of avoiding punishment and of obtaining rewards.[15] At the next 'transcendental' stage of moral realism a rule comes to be seen as a rule and to depend for its existence on the will of the peer-group and of authority figures. This is a crucial stage in moral development; for it involves the realisation on the part of the child of what it is to follow a rule, to accept a rule as a rule binding on one's conduct. Much of what Freud wrote about the super-ego is relevant surely to this stage, though he himself was concerned more with exaggerated and distorted types of 'internalisation' rather than with the normal developmental process of coming to accept a rule as a rule.[16] At this stage of development children come to enjoy following rules and to revel in the sense of mastery that this gives them. They have as yet no notion of the validity of rules. They regard them as just there, supported by the approval of the peer-group and of authority figures. It is a period at which imitation and identification are extremely important in learning.

This stage in rule-conformity is a very important one in moral development. In the U.S.S.R. Makarenko achieved considerable success in dealing with delinquents by reliance mainly on group projects and on identification with the collective will of the community.[17] If Piaget and Kohlberg are right, however, in their assumptions about the development of autonomy, *every* individual has to go through this stage of what Kohlberg calls 'good boy' morality before he can attain the autonomous stage. It is questionable whether progressive educators have been sufficiently aware of the importance of this second stage of development.

In the history of man development beyond this stage of morality to a third or autonomous stage is probably a rare phenomenon, depending on the development of what Popper has called an 'open society'. Within our own type of society Kohlberg himself stresses the differences in rate of development beyond the second stage of those who come from middle-class as distinct from working-class homes. There is, too, a series of investigations by Bruner and his associates, to which I have already referred,[18] which are far-reaching in their implications for the importance of social influences; for they show not only how individuals pass to the second stage, but also how they are massively discouraged from passing beyond it. In cultures such as that of the Wolof in Senegal there is no encouragement for the individual to develop independence, to explore the world 'for himself'. What is true is what the group, or the authority figure in the group, says.

This lasting attitude towards rules may not be just the product of vague social pressure and expectations; it may also be produced and perpetuated by the conscious techniques which we now call 'indoctrination'. For 'indoctrination' involves the passing on of fixed beliefs in a way which discourages questions about their validity. Societies like the U.S.S.R., in which indoctrination is widespread, are not societies in which reasoning in general is discouraged. What is discouraged is the particular form of reasoning which involves the questioning of the *validity* of moral and political beliefs and the placing of any emphasis on the role of the individual in determining his own destiny. They thus allow plenty of scope for the attitude to rules which is characteristic of Piaget's second stage but actively discourage any movement towards the autonomous stage, which they regard as an aberration of individualistic societies.

(c) *The Achievement of Autonomy*
So far I have sketched the sorts of social influences and techniques, such as indoctrination, which discourage people from passing beyond the second stage of 'good boy' morality. What is to be said about the type of influences that encourage development? It is difficult to say much even in a brief space about this because the notion of 'autonomy', which is the dominant feature of the third stage, is itself very complex.

There is, first of all, the notion of authenticity or genuineness. The suggestion is that a person accepts rules for himself, that his responses are not simply second-hand. Negatively this suggests that he is not just motivated by approval or disapproval from the peer-group or from authority figures. More positively it suggests that there must be some feature of a course of conduct, or of a situation, which constitutes a non-artificial reason for his decision or judgement, as distinct from extrinsic associations provided by praise and blame, reward and punishment, and so on, which are artificially created by the demands of others.

Secondly there is the aspect of autonomy stressed by Kant and Piaget – the ability to stand back and reflect on rules, and to subject them to criticism from the point of view of their validity and appropriateness. On Piaget's theory this is closely connected with reversibility of thought and with the ability to adopt the standpoint of others.

Thirdly there is the suggestion of strength of will, the ability to stick to a judgement or course of conduct in the face of counter-inclinations. These counter-inclinations often derive from motivations which consolidate conformity at previous stages – e.g. fear of punishment, disapproval and ostracism.

How, then, are these different aspects of autonomy developed? A general preliminary point must be made which is that we cannot expect young people to manage on their own unless they are given concrete opportunities to do so. This thought presumably lies behind the 'Outward Bound' movement and the Public Schools system of prefects. But such opportunities must be realistically related to responsibilities which it is reasonable for people to take. If too open a situation is created we are likely to get relapses back to and embeddedness in the second stage of morality due to the fear of freedom about which Eric Fromm has written so eloquently.[19]

Authenticity This conditional encouragement of the individual to strike out on his own is particularly important in the development of authenticity. There is a strange misconception that haunts the Socratic insistence that we should discover what we really want, which is that we can come to understand this before we actually try things out. But the truth is that we often only come to know what we genuinely want or feel *by* trying things out.

In the moral sphere 'authenticity' is closely connected with the capacity to experience compassion or concern for others in a first-hand way. For, as Hume put it, 'no action can be virtuous or morally good unless there be in human nature some motive to produce it distinct from the sense of its morality'.[20] To get beyond the second stage children must not do what is right just out of a 'sense of duty' or because it is the done thing. They must be sensitive to considerations, such as the suffering of others, in virtue of which actions are right or wrong. The findings of the Piaget school are that, at a very early age, children cannot grasp reasons for types of action in the sense that they cannot connect a practice such as that of stealing with considerations such as the harm to others brought about by such a a practice. In other words concern for others cannot serve as a *principle* for them. But this does not show that very early on they cannot genuinely feel concern for others. If they are sensitive to the suffering of others early on the hope is that, with the development of their capacity for reasoning, this will later be one of the main principles in a rational form of moral life.

How then do children come to feel concern for others? Is there an innate basis for it in sympathy? Is Money-Kyrle[21] right in arguing that the origins of what he calls the 'humanistic conscience' (Hume's 'sentiment for humanity'), which Freud neglected, are to be found in the child's early relationships with his mother? Does not this type of guilt need to be distinguished from the guilt which is the product of punishment and of internalised social disapproval? There is no answer to this type of question in the Piaget–Kohlberg theory. Yet a developmental account of concern for others is surely as important as a developmental account of reasoning and of the child's attitude to rules. In this area of moral development the findings of Piaget surely need to be supplemented by those of the Freudian and social learning schools of psychology. For there is considerable evidence to suggest that the child's capacity for sympathy and his trust in others depends very much on the pattern of his early social relationships.[22]

Reflection on Rules   What, then, in relation to the second aspect of autonomy, is to be done about the development of reasoning, so that considerations, such as concern for others, can serve as principles? Reasons for doing things can be indicated quite early on, even though it is appreciated that the child cannot yet think in this way. For without this type of 'cognitive stimulation' in the environment this reflective attitude to rules is unlikely to develop. I am not saying, of course, that any sane parent or teacher will, in the early stages, always make a child's acceptance of the reasons a condition for his doing what is sensible – e.g. refraining from playing on railway lines. This presumption is confirmed by the evidence from psychology; for the best established finding in this field is of the correlation between moral development and the use of techniques called 'induction', which cover explanation, pointing to the consequences of action, and so on.[23] There is also evidence that these techniques are ineffective until after the pre school years.[24] Language, too, which approximates to what Bernstein calls 'an elaborated code', is very important in aiding this development.[25]

Strength of Will   'Autonomy' suggests not simply reflection on rules but also following rules which have been accepted as the result of such reflection. To do this implies what psychologists call 'ego-strength' – the capacity to delay immediate gratification, or promptings of approval or disapproval, in favour of some more long-term, thought-out policy. The extent to which the development of this type of motivation, once closely associated with the Puritan ethic, depends upon specific types of social influences has been strongly argued by Bettelheim and others.[26] It is not just a matter of 'growth'. Even less so, probably, are virtues connected with strength of will such as courage, integrity and determination. These virtues are, perhaps, too little emphasised in recent times because of their association with more traditional moralities such as that of the English Public Schools. There are few, if any, empirical studies on how they are developed. Presumably habit-training is not unimportant in their development; for the peculiarity of these virtues is that they have to be exercised in the face of counter-inclinations. Unless, therefore, a child has some training in acting in the face of fear or anxiety, it seems probable that he will be overwhelmed by them if he encounters them at a later stage when attempting to take a line of his own. This was manifestly the assumption of educators in the Public School tradition who believed in some kind of transfer of training in this sphere. They tended, however, to stress too much the negative aspect of strength of will and neglected the sensitisation to positive considerations which give authentic and long-term point to resistance to fear or temptation.

(d)   *The Influence of Institutions*

So far I have been making suggestions about the ways in which individuals such as peers, parents and teachers can wittingly or unwittingly provide appropriate forms of 'cognitive stimulation' which help the development of a rational form of life. Nothing has been said about the all-pervasive influence of institutions which provide a potent source of latent learning for the growing child. Of particular significance is the general control system of the school and the motivational assumptions which support it. For Piaget's and Kohlberg's stages of development are 'writ large' in these all-pervasive features of an institution. It is unlikely that autonomy will be much encouraged by an authoritarian system of control in which anything of importance is decided by the fiat of the headmaster and in which the prevailing assumption is that the appeal to a man is the only method of determining what is correct. Similarly in the motivational sphere students are unlikely to develop a delight in doing things for reasons intrinsic to them if rewards and punishment, meted out both by the staff and by a fierce examination system, provide the stable incentives to the discipline of learning; for the institution itself embodies an attitude to conduct which is appropriate to Piaget's first stage of development. These institutional realities are bound to structure the perceptions of the students. If an institution embodies only an attitude to rules that is characteristic of an earlier stage of development, teachers who attempt to encourage a more developed attitude have an uphill task; for in their attempts at 'cognitive stimulation' they are working against the deadening directives of the institution.

The inference to be drawn from this is not that every school, which upholds an ideal of autonomy, should straightaway abolish its punishment and examination systems and introduce a school parliament which should direct the affairs of the institution in a way which is acceptable to autonomous man. Apart from the rational objections to the possibility of educational institutions being purely 'democratic'[27] it ignores the implications to be drawn from the Piaget–Kohlberg theory. For children have to pass from seeing rules as connected with punishments and rewards to seeing them as ways of maintaining a gang-given or authoritatively-ordained rule-structure before they can adopt a more autonomous attitude towards them. Kohlberg has shown that many adolescents are still only at the first 'pre-moral' stage, so the suggestion that an institution should be devised for them which is structured only in terms of the final stage is grossly inappropriate. Progressive schools, therefore, which insist *from the start* on children learning only what interests them, on making their own decisions and running their own affairs, ignore the crucial role which the stage of conventional morality plays in moral development. The more enlightened ones in fact have a firm authority structure for the school which is arranged so that increasing areas of discretion and participation in decision-making are opened up for the older pupils.

4 LEARNING THE CONTENT OF MORALITY

What, then, is to be said about learning the *content* of morality? For to date I have been concerned only with the learning of its form and have been stressing the role of various social influences in promoting what Kohlberg calls 'cognitive stimulation'. There are at least three questions which demand an answer. First, is the learning of a content necessary in moral education? Could not children just develop a form of thinking which enables them to work out a content for themselves? Secondly, if it is, what should this content be? Thirdly, *how* should it be learnt if development of a rational form of morality is to be encouraged?

(a) *Why Worry about Content?*

There is a kind of abstractness and unreality about the approach to moral education which places exclusive emphasis on the development of a rational form of morality and which considers its content unimportant, dismissing it, as Kohlberg does, as merely 'a bag of virtues'. To start with, even at an early age, children are capable of doing both themselves and others a lot of damage. Hobbes once noted a sobering feature of the human condition which is that a man can be killed by a small child while he is asleep. Also the hazards to small children in modern industrial society are innumerable. So for reasons both of social security and self-preservation, small children must be taught a basic code which, when internalised, will regulate their behaviour to a certain extent when they are not being supervised. There is also the point that a great number of people do not develop to a rational level of morality. For obvious social reasons, therefore, if the morality of such people is to be unthinking, its content is of crucial importance. If the ordinary citizen is mugged in the street, how the thief views rules about property is of academic interest to him.

But even if the focus is exclusively on the development of children rather than on these more palpable facets of social behaviour, there are logical absurdities about any cavalier disregard for content. In the first place, it is difficult to understand how a person could come to follow rules autonomously if he had not learnt, from the inside, as it were, what it is to follow a rule. And children learn this, presumably, by generalising their experience of picking up some particular 'bag of virtues'.

In the second place, how is the exercise of a principled form of morality to be conceived without reference to a determinate content? Respect for persons, for instance, as a principle is only intelligible in the context of a life in which people occupy roles, take part in activities and enjoy personal relationships. It suggests that people should not be treated just as the occupants of roles, that they should not be judged just for their competence in activities, and that, in more personal relationships they should not be used just as means to the purposes of others. Such a principle, in other words, sensitises the individual to the way in which he should conduct himself in the various areas of the moral life which constitute its content. It could not operate without such a concrete content. Indeed by calling something like respect for persons a 'principle' we mean that it embodies a consideration to which appeal is made when criticising, justifying or explaining some determinate content of behaviour or belief.

Usually a principle such as considering people's interests is appealed to in criticism or justification of a social practice such as abortion or punishment. But it can also be regarded as a τέλος immanent in roles and social practices. For parents, for instance, considering children's interests is one of the rationales underlying their role: indeed their role largely defines what this principle *means* in their dealings with their children. Most Utilitarians, too, have stressed the importance of Mill's 'secondary principles' in morality. The Utilitarian, Mill argued, has not to be constantly weighing up the effects of his action on people's interests any more than a Christian has to thumb through the Bible every time before he acts. The experience of a society with regard to the tendencies of actions in relation to people's interests lies behind its roles and rules. In a similar way concern for truth is to be conceived of as a τέλος underlying the procedures of science. If people practising activities and following rules are sensitive to such underlying principles they will adapt their behaviour sensitively to changes in circumstances. If, on the other hand, they are hide-bound traditionalists they may insist on conformity to the minutiae of a code that no longer has any point. But it is impossible to conceive of such a principled morality operating in a vacuum, divorced from a determinate content.

(b) *What Type of Content?*

Given then the indispensability of some kind of content for moral education the second question arises about the type of content which should constitute the basis of moral education. There is, as a matter of fact, a kind of unreality about this question if it is framed in too general a way. For, willy-nilly, adults will in fact introduce children in some way or other to the type of content which seems to them important. The world which the child has to inhabit is largely a social world structured by the roles, rules, activities and relationships of his parents, which will be shot through with the morality of his parents. The question, therefore, is which elements of this content are to be *emphasised* by parents. For the child will be exposed to it *in toto* and will pick much of it up by imitation and identification whatever their more explicit child-rearing techniques.

If parents subscribe to some form of the rational morality which I am assuming in this paper they will obviously emphasise, as soon as the child is ready, those considerations which are later to function as principles in a rational morality – e.g. fairness, consideration for others. They will also emphasise what I previously termed 'basic rules' such as those to do with contracts and property which can be defended as necessary to the continuance of any tolerable form of social life. What else could they rationally contemplate doing? For they could not hold that there were strong grounds for insisting on at least this minimum content of rules, under any conditions of social life and, at the same time, decline to insist on such rules in their own home.

(c) *How To Teach Content?*

The more interesting and controversial question is the third question relating to the manner rather than to the matter of early moral education. For how are they to emphasise these rudiments of moral-ity? The obvious answer, it might be thought, is by any method which is meaningful to the child at the stage of development at which he is. In moral education, surely, as in any other form of education, parents and teachers should begin where children are. This is obvious enough; but what is implies for moral learning is not obvious without more detailed analysis of the situation.

First, there is learning and learning. A rule could just be learnt as a bit of verbalism without any real understanding of its application. But obviously, because the function of moral rules is to regulate people's behaviour rather than just to act as incantations, a child must learn them in the sense of being able to apply them to a variety of situations. This means that he must attend to the situations and to the similarities in them picked out by the rule. Now many things can be learnt just by watching others – for instance simple skills, and reactions to situations. But moral rules could not be learnt just by a mixture of trial and error and watching what others do. For a com-plicated network of concepts, which structure social life, have to be understood. A child could not learn what 'borrowing', as distinct from 'stealing', is without a considerable amount of instruction and explanation.

It is inconceivable, for this reason too, that a child could learn to behave morally purely by some process of conditioning in the strict sense. He could not learn not to steal simply by some process of positive reinforcement; for he has to develop the concepts necessary to grasping *what* behaviour is being reinforced. This requires instruc-tion, explanation and other teaching methods by means of which *content* is marked out. Aids to learning, such as reinforcement, should not be confused with processes of learning.

Nevertheless, at the early stages of moral learning, aids to learning, which are developments of conditioning such as rewards and punishments, praise and blame, are extremely important. Indeed Piagetians claim, as has already been explained, that very small children can only see rules first of all as things to be done to avoid punishment or to obtain rewards, and then as forms of behaviour that are approved of or disapproved of by peers and authority figures. In the case of moral learning the importance of such extrinsic aids is not difficult to understand. For a child has not just got to learn how to apply concepts correctly; he has also to learn to behave consistently in the required way. Rules must regulate something and what they regulate are human inclinations. Children have, therefore, to start off their moral life with some kind of habit training. They may come to delight, at the second 'transcendental' stage of morality, in following rules; but often they do not do this because their counter-inclinations are strong. They want something now or they want something at other people's expense. Therefore insistence by parents or peer-groups on rules often has to be backed by extrinsic rewards and approval in order to provide positive incentives to out-weigh the pull of the child's inclinations. And so simple habits are built up, which constitute a basic 'bag of virtues'.

Parents, therefore, at these early stages have the option of supplementing example and instruction by the positive extrinsic aids of rewards or approval or by the negative ones of punishment and disapproval. There is strong evidence from psychological research which suggests that the positive aids are much more conducive to moral learning.[28] The reason for this can be related to the logic of the learning situation. If the child is going to learn, in the sense explained, he has to attend to the features of the situation, understand its point of similarity with other situations, and what his actions are likely to bring about. But, as is well known, attention is difficult to sustain under conditions of anxiety and stress or when someone is lacking confidence in his ability to understand. The hypothesis is that punitive and rejecting techniques militate against attention, and hence against learning, by producing anxiety, and undermine the child's confidence in himself. This explains, too, the lack of correlation between love-withdrawal and moral learning. For anxiety is produced by making the keeping of a mother's love contingent upon learning what 'being a good boy' consists in. Approval, on the other hand, together with parental warmth, which correlate well with moral learning, are thought to provide incentives for learning in a climate which is not fraught with anxiety.

5 TEACHING CONTENT IN RELATION TO THE DEVELOPMENT OF FORM

The use of such techniques has been considered so far on the assumption that what is being learnt is some content of morality. But an equally important way of looking at them is from the point of view of whether they aid or hinder the development of the rational form of morality. In this the validity of rules can be questioned and reasons for them discerned which fall under principles as distinct from their artificial associative connection with rewards and punishment, approval and disapproval. Obviously the use of induction is the most appropriate technique in so far as it involves, e.g. drawing attention to the consequences for others of a child's actions. But early on this type of technique makes little difference; for it is only when the child is capable of reversibility in thought and can look at actions from the point of view of others that this technique is effective. There are, understandably enough, no consistent findings relating to the effectiveness of induction in promoting moral development until after the pre-school years.[29] 'Induction', in the sense of teaching children rules, will obviously be effective. But in so far as it is concerned with trying to indicate to children the reasons for rules it will only be effective when they have reached the appropriate level of cognitive development.

These extrinsic aids to instruction and example, which have been discussed in the context of the learning of content, are also extremely relevant when the way the content is learnt is considered from the point of view of whether this learning situation is likely or not to promote a rational form of morality later on. It could well be, for instance, that many of the cases studied by psychologists of the Freudian school, of people who become fixated at an early stage of moral development with extreme irrational feelings of guilt and unworthiness about their conduct, are the victims of punitive and rejecting parental techniques. If children are to develop sensibly towards an autonomous form of morality they require a consistent pattern of rules in their early years, backed up by approval for learning. Interestingly enough, though, there is evidence to suggest that what Hoffman calls 'humanistic-flexible' individuals do emerge from homes in which parents, though relying on induction and approval, occasionally blow up and use power-assertive techniques.[30] This is quite different from the indiscriminate or systematic use of punishment. On occasions some assertion of power may be necessary for the voice of reason to be heard! Perhaps, too, there is some support for the wry advice that one should never strike a child save in anger!

Development is also likely to be stunted by complete permissiveness, whether this involves inconsistency in relation to what is expected or no determinate expectations; for the anxiety created by such inconsistency or anomie is not conducive to learning. Also under such conditions the child has little basis for predictability in his social environment which is necessary for anticipating consequences of actions. He gets little feed-back from his parents and interprets their 'liberal' policy as implying indifference to him. For children's conception of themselves, and their view of what it is possible for them to become, depends enormously on the messages about themselves that they read off from other people's expectations of them.

6 THE CHARGE OF INAUTHENTICITY

It might be objected that this willingness to use extrinsic aids such as rewards and approval is rather deplorable. It may not have disastrous consequences like the fierce use of punishment or disapproval. But will it not tend to ingrain in the individual a second-hand instrumental view of life? Will his moral life not be one of 'toil', lacking in authenticity? Would it not be better to rely on the more intrinsic motivations of delight in the mastery of rules and in the spontaneous co-operation exemplified by peer groups at play? Is not the content of morality more effectively picked up in these more spontaneous situations from older members of the peer group?

There is point in this criticism, but it represents altogether too idealistic a picture of what the situation actually is in peer-group co-operation. Certainly these intrinsic types of motivation exist, and are very important at the second stage of development. Certainly children learn much from others who are just a bit more advanced than they are – as the experiments of Turiel have shown.[31] But the pressure of social approval and disapproval is very strong in such situations. Indeed gang pressure on the individual can be much more oppressive than that of adults. Also disapproval for the unwilling or the incompetent is probably stronger than approval for the conformist. Furthermore, if an individual wishes to go his own way and to stand out against what is laid down by his peers, his situation is a parlous one unless there is some other source of approval, emanating from adults, which will support him in his strivings for independence.

The use of approval is surely on a par with the mechanisms of modelling and identification with adults which is equally important in transmitting moral content at this stage.[32] It depends on whether or not it is regarded as a transitional device. There is no evidence to suggest that these affectively charged links between the generations necessarily inhibit the development of autonomy. It depends entirely on how they are handled. The wise use of authority does not necessitate being authoritarian.

The question, too, has to be faced: what else is practicable? If children in their early years cannot acquire rules because they see the proper point of them and if, for the reasons explained, they have to start off with some 'bag of virtues', it is difficult to see what other alternatives are open. It should be stressed, however, that this early combination of 'induction' and positive 'reinforcement' does not constitute indoctrination; for 'indoctrination' picks out a special manner of instruction. It consists in getting children to accept a fixed body of rules by the use of techniques which incapacitate them from adopting a critical autonomous attitude towards them. Children are permanently fixated with a 'good boy' type of morality. They are perhaps led to associate obedience to such a fixed body of rules with loyalty to their group or to some authority figure whose disapproval they dare not incur. But not all instruction need employ such indoctrinatory techniques. Indeed it must not employ them if development towards a rational type of morality is to occur.

The crucial problem of methods in early moral education can, therefore, be stated in this way: given that it is thought desirable that children should develop an autonomous form of morality, and given that, if Piaget and Kohlberg are right, they cannot, in their early years, learn in a way that presupposes such an autonomous form, how can a basic content for morality be provided that gives them a firm basis for moral behaviour without impeding the development of a rational form of it? What non-rational methods of teaching aid, or at least do not impede, the development of rationality?

It is to this complex problem of instruction that sensitive parents and teachers should address themselves instead of withdrawing from the scene for fear of indoctrination. For by withdrawing and refusing to act as models and instructors they are equally in danger of impeding the development towards autonomy that they desire. It is indeed significant that Bronfenbrenner singles out the weakening of links between the generations, with the consequent lessening of opportunities for modelling and identification, as the main cause-factor in 'The Unmaking of the American Child'. 'Children', he says, 'used to be brought up by their parents'.[33]

REFERENCES

1. Much of the material of this paper is to be published elsewhere in books, especially in the author's Lindsay Memorial Lectures entitled *Reason and Compassion: Essays in Ethical Development* (London: Routledge & Kegan

Paul, 1973) and in a more popular paper entitled 'Form and Content in Moral Education' in the author's revised version of *Authority, Responsibility and Education* (London: Allen & Unwin, 1973).

2. See Peters, R. S., 'Freud's Theory of Moral Development in Relation to that of Piaget', *Brit. Journ. Ed. Psych.* Vol. XXX, Pt III (November 1960); and 'Moral Development: A Plea for Pluralism', in Mischel, T. (Ed.), *Cognitive Development and Epistemology* (New York: Academic Press, 1971).

3. See MacIntyre, A., *A Short History of Ethics* (London: Routledge & Kegan Paul, 1967).

4. See Peters, R. S., 'Reason and Passion', in Vesey, G. (Ed.), *The Proper Study*, Royal Institute of Philosophy Lectures, Vol. 4, 1969–70 (London: Macmillan, 1971).

5. See Hart, H. L. A., *The Concept of Law* (London: Oxford University Press, 1961), Ch. IX.

6. See Ginsberg, M., *Reason and Unreason in Society* (London: Longman, 1947), Ch. XVI; and *On the Diversity of Morals* (London: Heinemann, 1956), Ch. VII.

7. See Kohlberg, L., 'Stage and Sequence: the Cognitive–Developmental Approach to Socialisation', in Goslin, D., *Handbook of Socialisation Theory and Research* (Chicago: Rand McNally, 1969); and 'Education for Justice: A Modern Statement of the Platonic View', in Sizer, N. F. and Sizer, T. R. (Eds), *Moral Education* (Cambridge: Harvard University Press, 1970).

8. Piaget, J. *Six Psychological Studies* (London: University of London Press, 1968), pp. 8–17.

9. See Freud, S., *The Ego and the Id* (London: Hogarth Press, 1927).

10. See Greenfield, P. M. and Bruner, J. S., 'Culture and Cognitive Growth', in Goslin, D. (Ed.), *Handbook of Socialisation Theory and Research* (Chicago: Rand McNally, 1969).

11. See Peck, R. F. and Havighurst, R. J., *The Psychology of Character Development* (New York: John Wiley, 1970), pp. 109–11.

12. See Laing, R. D., *The Divided Self* (Harmondsworth: Penguin Books, 1965), p. 39.

13. For distinction see Peters, R. S. 'Reason and Passion' as in reference 4.

14. Klein, J. *Samples of Englich Culture* (London: Routledge & Kegan Paul, 1965), Vol. II.

15. Kohlberg divides this stage into two, avoidance of punishment preceding the seeking of rewards. Similarly the second stage of moral realism is subdivided into two – that of peer-group conformity and authority-based morality.

16. See Peters, R. S., 'Freud's Theory of Moral Development in Relation to that of Piaget', as in reference 2.

17. See Lilge, F., *Anton Semyonovitch Makarenko* (University of California Press, (1958), pp. 25–6).

18. Greenfield and Bruner, 'Culture and Cognitive Growth', as in reference 10.

19. Fromm, E., *The Fear of Freedom* (London: Routledge & Kegan Paul, 1942).

20. Hume D., *A Treatise of Human Nature*, Bk III, Pt II, Sec. I.

21. Money-Kyrle, R., *Psycho-analysis and Politics* (London: Duckworth, 1931).

22. See Hoffman, M. L., 'Moral Development', in Mussen, P. A., *Carmichael's Manual of Child Psychology* (New York: Wiley, 1970), Vol. 2, pp. 329–30, 346.

23. Ibid., pp. 302–3, 325.

24. Ibid., p. 325.

25. See Bernstein, B. B., 'Social Class and Linguistic Development: a Theory of Social Learning', in Halsey, A. H., Floud, J. and Anderson, C. A., *Education, Economy and Society* (New York: Free Press, 1961).
26. See Bettelheim, B., 'Moral Education', in Sizer, N. F. and Sizer, T. R. (Eds), *Moral Education* (Cambridge: Harvard University Press, 1970), Ch. 7.
27. See Hirst, P. H. and Peters, R. S., *The Logic of Education* (London: Routledge & Kegan Paul, 1970), Ch. 7.
28. See Hoffman, op. cit., passim.
29. Ibid., p. 325.
30. Ibid., p. 340.
31. See Turiel, E. 'Developmental Processes in the Child's Moral Thinking' in Mussen, P. A., Langer, J. and Corington, M. (Eds) *Trends and Issues in Developmental Psychology* (New York: Holt, Rinehart, & Winston, 1969).
32. For summary of some of the evidence see Bronfenbrenner, U., *Two Worlds of Childhood* (London: Allen & Unwin, 1971), pp. 124–43.
33. Bronfenbrenner, ibid., p. 95.

Chapter 8

The Place of Kohlberg's Theory in Moral Education*

A SKINNERIAN SCENARIO

Let me start with a thumb-nail sketch of B. F. Skinner's diagnosis of our moral malaise and the contours of its cure. In his view we have a large-scale problem of survival – not just economic but social as well. The fabric of society is threatened by violence, greed, theft, drug addiction, pollution, etc. Largely to blame are our thoroughly inefficient and superstitious ways of bringing up the young. Encouraged by the antiquated belief in our autonomy we make appeals to reason. These are supported by a mixture of permissiveness and punitive measures. Permissiveness only lays the child open to haphazard influences other than those of parents and teachers and punishment has been shown to be counter-productive in relation to learning.

The only scientifically supported alternative to our amateurish tinkering with the problem is the shaping of behaviour along socially desirable lines by a combination of systematic instruction in morals and modelling backed up by positive reinforcements. The social environment must be controlled and designed to encourage co-operative and socially useful forms of behaviour. Rules and practices that are essential to social survival must be singled out and instilled in the young by Skinnerian techniques. His recipe for salvation has much in common with the type of moral education practised in the U.S.S.R. as described by Bronfenbrenner in his *Two Worlds of Childhood*.[1]

There are obvious moral objections to such a programme which I

* This paper was read at an international conference on moral education and moral development held at Leicester University, 19–26 August 1977.

will not labour. Most of us, though perhaps believing autonomy to be rather an overworked virtue, would not dismiss it as a relic of the belief in a little man within a man; we would resist his attack on freedom and human dignity and the lack of respect for persons shown by both; and we might be sceptical at the superior value placed on happiness in the fancy dress of positive reinforcement. I propose to pass by such criticisms as too obvious to need development and to turn to the sort of psychological criticisms that might be made by someone like Kohlberg as a way of introducing his theory. I shall, however, return to Skinner's type of approach; for, as I shall hope to show, there are elements in it which are necessary supplements to Kohlberg's own approach.

KOHLBERG'S CRITICISMS

(i) Kohlberg claims, first of all, that Learning theorists have produced no positive evidence of the influence of early forms of habit training on adult behaviour.[2] Most of the evidence is negative – e.g. from studies of exposure to Boy Scouts, Sunday School, etc. and of early parental training in habits such as punctuality and neatness.[3] But Skinner would be unimpressed by such vague findings; for the techniques used were not made explicit, neither was there any systematic control of the patterns of reinforcement.

(ii) Of more substance would be Kohlberg's claim that this represents a 'bag of virtues' approach, an attempt systematically to instil in the young socially important virtues such as honesty and co-operation, which he claims are situation specific and not enduring traits of character. They depend very much on the continued presence of reinforcing agencies and are likely to collapse when those are absent. Kohlberg suggests that there is some evidence that they are stable if supported either by principles or by ego-strength or strength of will. The trouble about this criticism is that it is based on the controversial Hartshorne–May inquiry which dealt with a very limited number of virtues and, as I have argued elsewhere,[4] virtues are not all of a piece. Of particular importance is the fact that some are also motives for action, whereas others are not. Honesty, tidiness and punctuality, for instance, are not motives; they have no obvious reason for action built into them. It is not therefore surprising that they tend to be situation-specific depending upon what further reasons there may be for conforming to them, including the probability of rewards and punishment, approval or disapproval. Virtues like these are to be contrasted with gratitude, prudence and compassion which are also motives. They contain within themselves reasons for action which make them less strongly dependent on contextual considerations. Of course people may not act out of them because they deem some other feature of the situation to be more important. But if by 'important' is meant morally important this does not show that they are context-dependent.For virtues, as well as rules and principles, must be guarded by an 'other things being equal clause'. And other things are not equal if there is a conflict of duties situation.

There is another sense in which virtues are context-dependent which applies equally, if not more strongly, to the principles in which Kohlberg puts his trust. This is connected with variations of interpretation as to what is to *count* as stealing, cheating, dishonesty and the like. But as there are notorious difficulties about what is to count as justice (does one estimate it on the basis of need or merit, for instance?), or what is to count as people's interests, this type of difficulty has not to be faced only by those who want to make room for a 'bag of virtues' in morality in general and moral education in particular, to supplement the emphasis which Kohlberg places on principles.

(iii) Kohlberg's third and more fundamental criticism would be that Skinner is concerned only with moral learning, not with moral development. His techniques would have the effect of arresting people at the stage of conventional morality, without encouraging them to pass to the stage of principled morality.

KOHLBERG'S PROGRESSION

(a) *Logical Stages*

Kohlberg's defence of a principled morality and of the supreme importance of 'cognitive factors' is too well known to require exposition. I have worries about it on at least two scores. First, I think that it has difficulties internal to it. Second, because of the eloquence and voluminousness with which he has expounded it, it is very easy for the unsophisticated reader to be carried away and to think that the main ingredients of moral development have been revealed. Some constructive comment is therefore called for to protect Kohlberg against his own persuasiveness. For he would be the first to admit that his theory covers only part of the process of moral development.

My first batch of worries relates to the progression from stage to stage. I am not competent enough in empirical psychology to comment on the reliability and validity of the devices by means of which Kohlberg claims to have established them, as have Kurtines and Greif.[5] Neither can I do more than note with interest Gibbs's[6] recent contention that Kohlberg's first four stages satisfy Piaget type criteria of development but that the last two stages do not. My worry is more deep-seated; for Kohlberg claims that the stages form a hierarchical logical sequence, which implies that they logically must occur in the order which research has revealed them to occur.

If this were true the need for extensive research about the order of stages would seem superfluous; for they could be arrived at by reflection. To take a parallel, Piaget, after elaborate investigation of children, demonstrated the progression from concrete operations to formal operations. But Plato, in his brilliant allegory of the ascent from the cave, had already demonstrated this over two thousand years ago on the basis of a mixture of reflection and imagination. Similarly, in the moral sphere, it is difficult to see how an autonomous type of morality could precede a conventional one; for unless a child has had some prior introduction to rule-following and knows, from the inside, what it is to apply rules to his conduct, the notion of accepting or rejecting rules for himself, would scarcely seem intelligible. Kant's heteronomy and autonomy, which are the intellectual ancestors of Piaget's and Kohlberg's stages, were not postulated as the result of empirical investigation.

The trouble is, however, that this kind of conceptual truth does not manifestly apply to the details of Kohlberg's progression, even though he appeals to the logical hierarchy of stages to explain their cultural invariance. I can see no kind of logical necessity in the claim that the 'good boy' morality of the peer-group must precede a morality more dependent on the approval of authorities, for instance, in Stages Three and Four. There may be some kind of necessity for this, connected with the logical order of the concepts concerned; but Kohlberg has not made explicit what it is any more than he has made explicit, at Stages One and Two, why children must conceive of rules as connected with punishment before they see them as connected with rewards. I have raised this query before and still await Kohlberg's detailed demonstration of the alleged logical necessity.

Then there are Stages Five and Six, about which so little can be said because there are so few case studies of individuals that have reached them. About these stages I would be inclined to generalise Gibbs's thesis in that, once a person has achieved some kind of autonomy, and can reflect in a principled kind of way on rules, I can see no logical reason why he should not come up with any type of ethical position, rather than passing from a system characterised by an ideal order to one characterised by abstract principles. Whether reflective people embody their principles in ideal constructions like Hobbes's *Leviathan* or Rousseau's *Social Contract* or whether, like Sidgwick and Price, they formulate their principles in a more mundane abstract manner seems more to do with their imaginative and literary gifts than with their level of moral reasoning. And anyway what application has the notion of level of moral reasoning to those who have reached a stage at which they keenly dispute the priority of each other's principles? And what place are we to accord to an acute and abstract-minded sceptic such as David Hume who argued that morals depend not on rational principles but on disinterested passions?

My scepticism about the logical order of Kohlberg's stages, together with Gibbs's claims about the unsatisfactoriness of Stages Five and Six, and my own failure to see why reflection at the post-conventional stages should not lead to a pluralism of ethical positions, combine to attract me to Garbarino's and Bronfenbrenner's socialisation model[7] in which there are three stages resulting from the interaction between maturing capacities and motivations of the child on the one hand and particular characteristics of his socio-cultural milieu on the other. At the bottom is the amoral pattern with some primary hedonic principle of organisation such as self-interest or self-satisfaction. The second level includes all patterns of morality having as their dominant characteristic allegiance and orientation to some system of social agents. These include authority, peer and collective orientations. These are alternatives and may exist within and across cultures. They need not occur in any particular order in an individual. At the third level values, principles and ideas are the directing forces. This third level is Kohlberg's Stages Five and Six without the emphasis on the principle of justice. For this level to emerge a very special set of social conditions are required.

(b) *Cognitive Stimulation*

My other worry about the progression from stage to stage relates to the distinction that Kohlberg makes between 'teaching' and 'cognitive stimulation'. He holds that the *content* of moral rules can be taught but the attitude to them characteristic of the various stages cannot. It is a matter of the child's interaction with the social environment aided by 'cognitive stimulation'. But as he takes

Socrates' method of bringing the young to grasp principles as a method of cognitive stimulation he is obviously employing a very narrow concept of 'teaching'; for in any straightforward sense Socrates was teaching the slave in *Meno* all right, even though he was not telling him anything. By 'teaching' he seems to mean direct instruction and it is obvious enough why the view of rules that characterises the different stages could not be imparted in this way. For it is not a memory task nor the acquisition of a skill. The learner has to catch on; the penny has to drop. And this comes about by being put in the way of plenty of examples with appropriate stimulation from others – e.g. in questioning, role-playing, etc. What is not clear, however, is what else might be cognitively stimulating. Kohlberg claims that the peer-group – especially those at a slightly higher level – are an important source of 'cognitive stimulation'. But is the modelling that goes on in such groups as well as the discussion and role-playing a source of such stimulation? Does exposure to TV help? And so on. I find the concept of 'cognitive stimulation' reasonably straightforward when it is used to describe a group of methods for getting a child to grasp a principle like that of conservation in Piagetian experiments. But I do not find it very easy to pin down in the contexts in which children acquire different orientations to rules, except, of course, in the experiments done with children under controlled conditions by Turiel and Rest.[8]

THE AFFECTIVE ASPECTS OF MORALITY

The crown of Kohlberg's moral system is the principle of justice. Considering the importance which he attaches to it, he is very elusive in his treatment of it. Sometimes it appears in the skeleton form of Hare's prescriptivity and universalisability. At other times it is fleshed out with references to freedom and human welfare. Sometimes reciprocity and respect for persons are thrown in. And so on. But I do not want to enter into details of Kohlbergian exegesis; I want rather to make two points about his treatment which open up a whole vista of moral development with which his system does not deal, namely the *affective* aspects of development.

When Kohlberg talks of the principle of justice, it is not clear whether he has in mind the very formal principle that no distinctions should be made unless there are relevant differences or more concrete versions of it in distributive or commutative justice. But *any* application of this principle must involve a love of consistency and a hatred of arbitrariness. What is the developmental history of this sense of justice? Kohlberg, like Piaget, postulates a striving for 'equilibration' which leads children to assimilate and accommodate. This is the main motivation for development. I have elsewhere[9] tried to show that this biological metaphor is unnecessary. What Piaget is talking about is the striving for consistency. This may be necessary but it surely is not sufficient when we are dealing with the motivational side of moral development and not just with intellectual development. What is missing?

(a)   *Consideration for Others*

The clue to what is missing can be found, I think, by returning to the principle of justice. For justice is, as it were, the principle of principles, which may have led Kohlberg to have accorded it such pre-eminence. In its minimal form of impartiality it holds that no exceptions are to be made to a principle unless there are relevant grounds. In its more full-blooded form it demands impartial consideration of people's claims and interests. The point is that it cannot be employed unless something *else* of value is at stake. For unless there is some other criterion of value how do we determine relevance? Questions of justice, too, simply do not arise unless something of value has to be distributed or exchanged. Usually what is at stake is people's welfare or interests. It is no accident that occasionally Kohlberg slips in some reference to human welfare when he talks about his higher stages. So we have at least one more fundamental principle in the system – the consideration of people's interests. (I will not tease Kohlberg by calling it the virtue of benevolence!) I happen to think that this fundamental principle is as important in morality as the principle of justice. Yet there is no proper genetic account of it in either Piaget or Kohlberg, presumably because of their Kantian ancestry. It is true that Piaget gives an ingenious account, in terms of role-taking, of how the development of concrete operations coincides with the ability to take the point of view of another. But he never shows why a child should *care* about the other whose point of view he can take. And this is what requires explanation. The question is whether some account can be given of it which is a congenial supplement to the Piaget–Kohlberg story.

McPhail's *Lifeline* programme[10] makes caring for others the pivotal point of his material. But he was concerned with devising suitable teaching material for adolescents, not with a developmental progression. Indeed his emphasis on the rewarding character of this type of behaviour to the individual who practises it, suggests that he is catering for those not far advanced in Kohlberg's stages. But he is surely right in emphasising 'consideration for the needs, feelings and interests of others' in morality even if he rather underplays the importance of more rational principles such as justice.

But what of the *developmental* aspect of this principle with which neither McPhail nor Kohlberg deals? Recently Martin Hoffman has suggested a developmental theory of altruism which is consistent with Piagetian principles.[11] As his theory may be unfamiliar to many I will sketch its rough outlines. His assumption is that man is innately capable of both egoistic and altruistic motivation and his aim is to propose a theory of how the latter may develop in the individual. The basis of his theory is the human capacity to experience the inner state of others who are not in the same situation. It begins with empathy, the involuntary experiencing of another's emotional state. He suggests classical conditioning paradigms to explain this, either in terms of early transfer of tension from the caretaker to the child, or in terms of the unpleasant effect accompanying one's own painful past experiences which is evoked by another person's distress cues which resemble the stimuli associated with the observer's own experiences. These explanations are highly controversial. Irene Sebastian and Thomas Wren, for instance, in a yet unpublished paper,[12] challenge the thesis that altruism is thus based on an historically prior egoism, point to implausibilities in the conditioning explanations, and suggest intrinsic altruistic motivation from the start, which is innate. But this is not the place to enter into an age old controversy dating back to Hobbes, Butler and Hume.

Whatever the origin of this response the next important stage comes when the infant is capable of grasping object-permanence, especially that of persons. Empathy or sympathy can then be felt for someone whom the child appreciates as being distinct from himself – usually his mother – although, on Piaget's view the child's outlook is still basically ego-centric. The next crucial step is when the child's ego-centricism gives way to role-taking and the child begins to realise that others have different points of view. Piaget puts this stage quite late – at seven to eight years. But Hoffman argues that in familiar and highly motivating natural settings rudiments of role-taking may begin several years earlier. It culminates in an awareness by the child that others have their own personal identity, their own life circumstances and inner states. (This proceeds with his sense of his own personal identity and distinctiveness.) So the child would continue to react to the momentary distress of others but would feel worse if he knew that it was chronic. With further cognitive development the person may acquire the capacity to comprehend the plight not only of an individual but also of an entire group or class to whom he is exposed – rather like Hume's postulated transition from 'limited benevolence' to 'the sentiment for humanity'. Hoffman produces a certain amount of evidence to support the direct connection between altruistic motivation and action, though he admits that this is more likely when the appropriate thing to do is obvious. He stresses, however, the costs to the observer and the strength of competing motives aroused in him by the situation – especially in an individualistic society.

Hoffman suggests four hypotheses about experiences that may help to foster altruistic motivation:

(i) Allowing the child to have the normal run of distress experiences rather than shielding him from them.
(ii) Providing the child with opportunities for role-taking and for giving help and responsible care to others.
(iii) Encouraging the child to imagine himself in the place of others.
(iv) Exposure for a long time to loved models who behave altruistically.

This is a suggestive, if speculative, story about how we may come to care about others. It suffers, however, from a certain kind of coarseness in that, for instance, the concern felt by a boy for the suffering of one of his gang surely differs qualitatively from that felt by an adolescent for someone whom he knows more intimately as an individual. It may be possible, equally speculatively, to refine this account a bit by making use of some work done by Secord and Peevers[13] on children's perception of others. For emotional responses depend always on a cognitive core, on how the situation is perceived, especially other people in it. More refinement on the cognitive side of Hoffman's theory should have the effect not only of introducing more qualitative distinctions but also of bringing it closer to the Piaget–Kohlberg type of framework. For this was the type of framework that Secord and Peevers used.

They found, for instance, under the aspect of ego-involvement in descriptions of others, that most descriptions used by kindergarten children were saturated with references to the other person's attitude to themselves. Seventh-grade children, on the other hand, tended to use descriptions involving mutuality. 'We' or 'us' occurred frequently. The other person was regarded, as it were, as a comrade. At the eleventh grade predominant use is made of other-oriented items.

The most dramatic feature of the findings was the growth of the use of other-oriented terms with age, although ego-centric and mutual items appear at all ages.

Depth of description was another important developmental dimension. The child starts at Level One with simple descriptions locating a person in terms of his possessions, role, social setting, superficial qualities and global characteristics. At Level Two descriptions are more sophisticated, involving contradictory or amusing characteristics, conditions under which the other person exhibits qualities, references to trying, etc. At Level Three *explanations* of characteristics begin to appear. These types of causal-genetic descriptions are rare and do not begin to appear until the high school and college level.

If we transpose these findings about the perception of others to the cognitive aspect of consideration for others, they would suggest that early on sympathetic responses are likely to be tinged with egocentricity. Children would be more likely to respond in this way to those who liked or loved them. This would be followed by the stage of mutuality, Piaget's stage of realism. Others would be regarded as pals; there would be loyalty to comrades. Sympathy for others would not be highly personalised but would be directed towards an individual as a member of the same group. A feeling of fraternity would overlay responses to individuals. At the final level sympathetic reaction to another in distress would be to him as an individual in his own right. Questions of motive and understanding in depth would make the response more discriminating and a degree of objectivity in attitude would supersede the earlier overlays of egocentricity and mutuality. Disinterested care for another human being as a person would be possible, even though it might, at times, be tinged with traces of the earlier attitudes of egocentricity and mutuality.

I appreciate only too well that this account is no more than what Plato called a 'likely story' though it takes the form, not of a myth, but of a report of a limited number of psychological studies. It does have the merit, however, of being more or less consistent with the Piaget–Kohlberg view of cognitive development. As effect does not float about in us unattached but is dependent upon our interpretations of the world and other people, if there is any truth in the Piaget–Kohlberg developmental account, the affective supplement to it must be something like this in rough outline. In a previous publication[14] I actually suggested a very similar account of stages of understanding other people before I had ever read Secord and Peevers!

(b) *Negative Motivations*

The affective aspect of morals covers not only positive motivations such as sympathy and consideration for others: it includes also more negative ones such as shame and guilt. The most straightforward of these, from Kohlberg's or anyone else's point of view, is shame. For this is the emotion most characteristic of transgressors at what he calls the 'good boy' stage of morality. It is felt by the individual who is conscious that he has let the side down, or not lived up to what is expected of him in the sight of his peers. As Rawls has pointed out[15] there is a close connection between shame and self-respect. One can feel ashamed of one's appearance or slow-wittedness which is natural shame. Moral shame is occasioned by falling short of virtues that a person's plan of life encourages. The self is diminished and usually other people, who draw attention to such shortcomings, are the main agents of this feeling of self-diminishment. Kohlberg actually makes no mention of shame in his chart of 'Motives for Engaging in Moral Action'.[16] But he could easily have included it in Stage Three or Four.

Guilt is much more difficult to deal with because of the voluminous writings about it by the Freudian School, set in motion by the concept of the super-ego. But whether an account is given in terms of identification and introjection, or whether a social learning theory such as that of Aronfreed[17] is adopted, it seems undeniable that quite early on children internalise rules, the breaking of which occasions a feeling of guilt. This is often called 'authority guilt', because the prohibitions, on account of their source, are likely to be tinged with other natural emotions such as fear and anxiety, on account of the possibility of punishment or of the withdrawal of love. Presumably, in Piagetian terms, it begins to manifest itself when the child is passing to the stage of moral realism, when he sees rules as Durkheim put it, *comme les choses*, and not just egocentrically.

This, however, is only one type of guilt which may be prevalent in certain types of societies. In the psycho-analytic literature another type of guilt has been postulated. Money-Kyrle,[18] for instance, who owed much to Melanie Klein, claimed that Freud's theory was one-sided because it dealt only with the authoritarian conscience. There is also the humanistic conscience which has its origin in the 'guilt' experienced in hating and hurting the mother, the first object of the child's love. In its earliest form it would surely be somewhat imprecise to call this 'guilt', as 'guilt' presupposes acting contrary to one's sense of right and justice. And infants can scarcely be credited with such concepts. Nevertheless, if there is anything in such a hypothesis – and who can cross their heart and say honestly that they understand what is meant to be going on when they read the writings of Klein, Fairbairn, Guntrip, *et al.* – it would provide a fitting negative parallel to the Hoffman hypothesis about the origins of altruism. The point is that in guilt we tend to focus on the infringement of claims of others and on injuries done to them, whereas in shame we are more sensitive to our *own* loss of self-esteem and our disappointment in being unable to live up to our ideals. So though there is 'authority guilt' in which doing wrong is associated with anxiety and fear of punishment from parents or parent-substitutes, there must also be some origin to straightforward guilt which is not so associated, and which is what we feel when we injure others or infringe some accepted rule such as that of honesty or promise-keeping. Whether we feel guilt or shame when we fail to live up to Kohlberg's principle of justice depends on how self-referentially we view it. We may even feel remorse which seems to be a mixture of guilt at wrong-doing and shame that we could be the sort of person to do such a wrong.

THE CONTENT OF MORALITY

So much for speculations about the affective side of moral development which I have tried to make consistent with Kohlberg's cognitive theory. I pass now to a few observations about the content of morality which is the other glaring omission in Kohlberg's scheme. This omission is not one of inadvertence; for he repeatedly says that a 'bag of virtues' is unimportant in a person's moral equipment. It must first be remarked that he has quite a bag himself at Stages Five and Six which make them quite unlike earlier stages where rules are linked to general attitudes such as approval of authority figures and peers, reward and punishment. When he comes to the principled stage of morality, justice, human welfare, respect for persons and society appear as principles. But why just these? A principle is merely a consideration to which we appeal in order to justify a rule or practice. Promise-keeping would be functioning as a principle, for instance, if it was used to justify a person's refusal to entertain divorce. Presumably Kohlberg has in mind those principles which are fundamental to the use of reason, for which it is difficult to argue that further reasons can be given. Why not then include truth-telling? For Peter Winch[19] has argued that this principle is a presupposition of human communication. This may be too strong a thesis actually; but a good case can be made out for it as a presupposition of the descriptive, explanatory, and argumentative uses of language, which would include moral reasoning. At the principled level of morality Kohlberg would then have quite a formidable 'bag of virtues' – justice, benevolence, respect and truth-telling.

But what of his claims for the unimportance of lower level content which can be justified by appeal to such principles? Well, the first and obvious points to make are logical ones:

(i) It is very important that children should firmly internalise a set of rules so that they know what it is to act on a rule in a non-egocentric fashion. Unless they do this they have not the necessary basis to reflect on rules in the light of principles and to accept or reject those which they deem justifiable or non-justifiable.

(ii) Content vitally affects the application of principles both in the lives of societies and individuals. What counts as welfare, for instance, depends very much on current social practices and individual needs (a normative notion). The application of justice depends on whether need is thought more important than desert. And so on. There is no slide-rule for applying abstract principles to concrete situations. How they are applied, which is often highly controversial, depends upon judgment and what Kohlberg calls the 'content' of morality in a given society. And unless there were a determinate content principles would have no function; for they are what we appeal to when we criticise or justify some lower-level form of conduct.

I pass now to more practical considerations that concern us as parents, teachers and citizens. Thomas Hobbes once made the sobering remark that even a small child can kill a grown man while he is asleep. His fearful imagination conjures up a picture of a home in which the children set fire to the curtains, break all the windows and torture the cat. Why is not such exuberance more common? For the parents cannot be ever-present supervisors. Presumably because the children have internalised a set of rules which inhibit them from doing certain things. The same applies to schools, though in certain areas teachers have an uphill task in getting children to observe a reasonable code of conduct. We are in the same boat as citizens; for given that every underground and dark alley cannot be patrolled by the police and given that, on Kohlberg's figures, only a very small minority of the population reach his stage of principled morality, it is absolutely essential that the vast majority get well bedded down in a basic code at Stages Three and Four. For if you are assaulted and have your wallet taken it is the content of the assailant's code that matters to you, not speculations about whether he has passed from Stage One to Two.

The point is that there are certain basic rules of content, in addition to Kohlberg's principles, such as keeping your contracts, preserving property whether public or private, not stealing, the general observance of which is essential to the maintenance of social life under almost any conceivable conditions. These can be straightforwardly justified by an appeal to Kohlberg's principles and are in a different category from controversial rules like those relating to sexual practices and Trade Unions. It is absolutely essential that in this area of basic rules there should be a high degree of conformity, whether people conform on principled grounds or whether their conformity is of the conventional type. We cannot rely just on the law.

Kohlberg admits that, though progression from stage to stage cannot be directly taught, content can be. And so we return full circle to the picture presented at the start by Skinner and his advocacy of systematic teaching of basic social virtues backed up by positive reinforcement. Now I am not a Skinnerian. Indeed I have been very critical all my academic life not just of Skinner[20] but of Behaviourism generally as a movement in psychology.[21] But I do see virtue in the systematic holding up of standards to young children, backed up by approval. I do see virtue in the modelling advocated by Social Learning theorists and the kind of atmosphere in the home and infant school which permits the use of what Hoffman[22] calls 'induction', which is a kind of elementary moral instruction. Maybe, as Hoffman claims, some mild forms of power assertion are necessary as well to draw attention to what is important. But it should not be severe so that learning is constantly inhibited by fear and anxiety. I see virtue in these sorts of techniques not just because of the evidence produced by Hoffman and others but because, if Piaget and Kohlberg are right about the early stages of morality, there is no other way that a rule is meaningful to a small child as a guide to conduct except as linked with approval and disapproval, reward and punishment. There would be no point in general in having such rules, unless they regulated wayward inclinations, so conformity usually demands the presence of some counter-inclination such as the desire for approval or reward, as at this age the child cannot see their point deriving from principles.

At the same time, of course, there will be encouragement of the sense of justice and concern for others that are *later* to serve as principles if the child gets to the principled stage. The problem of moral education, on this view, is how to encourage these embryonic principles and how to teach a basic content so that Kohlberg's progression will take place. Some techniques, which we call indoctrination, fixate a person at his 'good boy' stage and positively discourage him from passing to a stage at which the content which has been absorbed will be reflected upon critically in the light of principles. And are those people, popularised by the Freudian school, who become fixated at an early stage with extreme feelings of guilt and unworthiness about their conduct, victims of punitive and rejecting parental techniques of child-rearing? Development is equally likely to be stunted by permissiveness, whether this involves indeterminacy in relation to what is expected or no determinate expectations; for the anxiety created by such conditions of inconsistency or anomie are not conducive to learning. Also there is little predictability in such an environment which is essential for learning to grasp the consequences of actions, and the child gets little feed-back from parents, which he interprets as indifference. I would hazard the guess that self-esteem, which is later connected with shame, is one of the most important factors in moral character. On some views it is closely connected with will or 'ego-strength', the importance of which Kohlberg admits. But self-esteem depends enormously on the messages about them which children read off from ways in which they are treated; it is not just, as Freudians have argued, a matter of internalising the qualities of admired adults.

It may well be that this content is, to a certain extent, situation specific. But so are high-order principles such as justice, the consideration of others, and truth-telling, in that differing social contexts as well as judgment are involved in their application. It may be that there is much inconsistency and back-sliding in following a code of conduct that constitutes the content of morality. But the degree of this will depend upon the degree of continuity in the presence of reinforcers such as approval. The same applies to a principled morality if it is not backed up by strength of will, which can also help, as Kohlberg admits, at the level of content.

Of course the stage of conventional morality has its defects. I am not arguing for its moral superiority – only for its logical necessity and practical necessity in any account of the moral life. I am insisting that more thought needs to be given to its content and to the methods by which it is taught. For given that small children cannot see the rationale for it in terms of principles, and given that, for the reasons which I have outlined, they have to learn such a basic code, the problem is to employ methods of teaching it to them, which are effective without being indoctrinatory, and which prepare the way for a principled morality later. If parents and teachers withdraw too much and refrain from acting as models we are likely to get the sort of phenomena described by Bronfenbrenner in his chapter on 'The Unmaking of the American Child'.[23] If they are too authoritarian and punitive we are likely to get individuals who are indoctrinated or crippled with irrational guilt. What we want to know is the middle road that is likely to lead to Kohlberg's heroes such as Martin Luther King.

REFERENCES

1. Bronfenbrenner, U., *Two Worlds of Childhood* (London: Allen & Unwin, 1971), Chs 1 and 2.
2. Kohlberg, L., 'Moral Education in the Schools', *School Review*, Vol. 74, (1966), pp. 1–30.
3. Kohlberg, L., 'Development of Moral Character and Ideology' in Hoffman, M. L. (Ed.), *Review of Child Development Research*, Vol. 1 (New York: Russell Sage Foundation, 1964).
4. Peters, R. S., 'Moral Development: a Plea for Pluralism' in Peters, R. S., *Psychology and Ethical Development* (London: Allen & Unwin, 1974).
5. Kurtines, W. and Greif, E. B., 'The Development of Moral Thought: Review and Evaluation of Kohlberg's Approach', *Psychol. Bull.*, Vol. 81, No. 8 (August 1974).
6. Gibbs, J. C., 'Kohlberg's Stages of Moral Judgment: a Constructive Critique', *Harvard Ed. Rev.*, Vol. 47, No. 1 (February 1977).
7. Garbarino, J. and Bronfenbrenner, U., 'The Socialization of Moral Judgment and Behaviour in Cross-cultural Perspective' in Lickona, T. (Ed.), *Moral Development and Behaviour* (New York: Holt, Rinehart & Winston, 1976).
8. Turiel, E., 'An Experimental Test of the Sequentiality of Developmental Stages in the Child's Moral Judgements', *J. Personal. Soc. Psy.*, Vol. 3, (1966), p. 611–18; Turiel, E., 'Developmental Processes in the Child's Moral Thinking' in Mussen, P. H., Langer, J. and Covington, M. (Eds), *Trends and Issues in Developmental Psychology* (New York: Holt, Rinehart & Winston, 1969); and Rest, J., 'Patterns of Preference and Comprehension in Moral Judgements', *J. Personality*, Vol. 41 (1973), pp. 86–109.
9. Peters, R. S., 'The Development of Reason' in Peters, R. S., *Psychology and Ethical Development* (London: Allen & Unwin, 1974).
10. McPhail, P., Ungoed-Thomas, J. R. and Chapman, H., *Moral Education in the Secondary School* (London: Longman, 1972).
11. Hoffman, M. L., 'Empathy, Role-taking, Guilt and Development of Altruistic Motives' in Lickona, T. (Ed.), *Moral Development and Behaviour* (New York: Holt, Rinehart & Winston, 1976).
12. Sebastian, I. and Wren, T., 'The Origin of the Altruistic Response', unpublished.
13. Secord, P. F. and Peevers, B. H., 'The Development of Person Concepts' in Mischel, T. (Ed.), *Understanding Other Persons* (Oxford: Blackwell, 1974).
14. Peters, R. S., 'Personal Understanding and Personal Relationships' in Mischel, T. (Ed.), *Understanding Other Persons* (Oxford: Blackwell, 1974).

15. Rawls, J., *A Theory of Justice* (Harvard: Harvard University Press, 1971), p. 444.
16. Kohlberg, L., 'From is to Ought' in Mischel, T. (Ed.), *Cognitive Development and Epistemology* (New York: Academic Press, 1971).
17. Aronfreed, J., 'Moral Development from the Standpoint of a General Psychological Theory' in Lickona, T. (Ed.), *Moral Development and Moral Behaviour* (New York: Holt, Rinehart & Winston, 1976), p. 170.
18. Money-Kyrle, R., *Psycho-analysis and Politics* (London: Duckworth, 1951).
19. Winch, P., 'Nature and Convention', *Proc. Aristotelian Soc.*, reprinted in Winch, P., *Ethics and Action* (London: Routledge & Kegan Paul, 1972).
20. See 'Survival or the Soul' in Peters, R. S., *Psychology and Ethical Development* (London: Allen & Unwin, 1974).
21. See op. cit. Chs 1 and 2 and Peters, R. S., *The Concept of Motivation* (London: Kegan Paul, 1958).
22. See Hoffman, M. L., 'Moral Development' in Mussen, P. A. (Ed.), *Carmichael's Manual of Child Psychology*, Vol. 2, passim. (New York: Wiley, 1970).
23. See Bronfenbrenner, U., *Two Worlds of Childhood* (London: Allen & Unwin, 1971).

Index